ESSENTIAL
MEDICAL LAW

Cavendish
Publishing
Limited

London • Sydney

Titles in the series:

Company Law
Constitutional Law
Contract Law
Criminal Law
Employment Law
English Legal System
European Community Law
Evidence
Family Law
GCSE Law
Jurisprudence
Land Law
Medical Law
Succession
Tort Law
Trusts

ESSENTIAL
MEDICAL LAW

Brendan Greene, LLB, MA
Senior Lecturer in Law
University College Northampton

Cavendish
Publishing
Limited

London • Sydney

First published in Great Britain 2001 by Cavendish Publishing Limited, The Glass House, Wharton Street, London WC1X 9PX, United Kingdom

Telephone: +44 (0)20 7278 8000   Facsimile: +44 (0)20 7278 8080

Email: info@cavendishpublishing.com

Website: www.cavendishpublishing.com

British Library Cataloguing in Publication Data

Greene, Brendan
Medical law – (Essential law series)
1 Medical laws and legislation – Great Britain
I Title
344.4'1'041

ISBN 1 85941 546 6

Printed and bound in Great Britain

Foreword

This book is part of the Cavendish Essential series. The books in the series are designed to provide useful revision aids for the hard-pressed student. They are not, of course, intended to be substitutes for more detailed treatises. Other textbooks in the Cavendish portfolio must supply these gaps.

Each book in the series follows a uniform format of a checklist of the areas covered in each chapter, followed by expanded treatment of 'Essential' issues looking at examination topics in depth.

The team of authors bring a wealth of lecturing and examining experience to the task in hand. Many of us can even recall what it was like to face law examinations!

Professor Nicholas Bourne AM
General Editor, Essential Series
Conservative Member for Mid and West Wales
Spring 2001

Preface

Medical law provides a uniquely challenging area of study, because of both its intellectual demands and the fact that, by its nature, it will have an impact on our individual lives. This book has two aims: first, to provide an introduction and overview of the main legal and ethical issues arising in medical law; and, secondly, to provide a revision aid for the student facing examinations.

The book explains the main principles of medical law and includes important legislation, cases and extracts from codes of conduct. Reference is made to academic articles, journals and standard academic works throughout the text.

The book may also serve as an introduction to the subject for those who work in the medical field, including staff in the National Health Service.

My thanks are due to the staff at Cavendish Publishing for their support in writing this book, and in particular to Ruth Massey. I have endeavoured to state the law as it stood on 1 January 2001.

Brendan Greene
January 2001

Contents

1 Introduction to Medical Law

You should be familiar with the following areas:

- deontological and utilitarian theories
- distinctions between civil and criminal law; the courts likely to be used in medical law; claims in contract; judicial review
- human rights and Articles of the European Convention on Human Rights (incorporated in Sched 1 to the HRA 1998)

Introduction

Medical law touches the lives of everyone and raises fundamental questions about life, death and many of the things which happen in between those two events in peoples' lives. The law attempts to deal with a wide range of problems, such as what to do with patients who refuse treatment or patients who are unable to consent to treatment; how to respond to the increasing number of claims for medical negligence; and what rights children have in respect of treatment. There are many contemporary issues with which the law has to grapple, including whether there should be an automatic right to abortion, when organs may be removed from dead patients and whether to legalise the practice of euthanasia. The ethical and legal dilemmas have recently been highlighted by the discovery of the practice of removing organs from dead children at Alderhey Hospital in Liverpool and at Bristol Royal Infirmary and by the case of the conjoined twins, Jodie and Mary.

Ethical theories and principles

Medical law is not simply a set of rules which can be applied to solve legal problems, because it frequently involves questions of morals – whether particular actions are the right thing to do – for example, the issue of abortion. Ethical rules are important because ethical principles sometimes underpin legal rules; for example, the law on consent to treatment is based on the principle of autonomy. Sometimes, there are no legal rules, or the rules are unclear and decisions have to be made on the basis of ethical principles, for example, if tissue is taken from a dead body. There is also the question of individual moral perspectives – clearly, the law cannot satisfy everyone, as people have conflicting moral views. What should the role of the law be in such conflicts? Should it be a matter for the individual to decide, or should the law impose limits on people's rights? Again, the example of abortion may be used. A second example is the conflict between the parents of Jodie and Mary, who did not want the twins to be separated, and the doctors at St Mary's Hospital, Manchester, who *did* want to separate the twins.

There are two main ethical theories: deontological – which is based on what is the right thing to do in any particular circumstances; and utilitarianism – which aims broadly to maximise happiness and evaluates an action on the consequences of that action:

- Deontological theory: 'deon' means duty and this approach determines whether an action is right by asking if there is a duty to do it or not, for example, a duty not to kill. Immanuel Kant was a proponent of this theory and believed that it could be used to judge whether any particular act was morally right or wrong. This approach tends to look for principles which can be followed, for example, the principle of autonomy. Autonomy means 'self-rule' and its wider meaning is to think and act freely. In a medical context, the doctor would be under a duty to respect the patient's autonomy.

- Utilitarian theory: this judges an action by what its consequences are, with the aim of maximising happiness. Jeremy Bentham and JS Mill were exponents of this theory. It can be seen as a 'goal-based' approach, the goal being to maximise the benefit, or welfare, to society. An action is right if it has good consequences and the nature of the action does not matter. It does not take a stand on principle but simply looks at the consequences. For example, it would not consider abortion wrong in itself because it offends the principle of the 'sanctity of life', but would judge it on its overall effect on society. A utilitarian approach will breach duties and violate rights if this maximises the good.

Apart from ethical theories, there are a variety of moral principles which play an important part in medical law and ethics. These include the principles of autonomy, beneficence (to do good), non-maleficience (to do no harm) and justice (to treat people fairly). The traditional approach in medicine was based on the principle of beneficence, in that doctors saw their role as helping patients. All too often, this became 'doctor knows best' and many doctors took a paternalistic approach to their patients. Over the last 30 years, patients' rights have grown more important and the principle of autonomy has come to the fore.

The wider context of medical law

Civil and criminal law

Although medical law is now recognised as a separate branch of law, it must be remembered that it operates in the wider context of the legal system. The distinction between civil and criminal law must be borne in mind and, although most matters of medical law will be civil ones, the criminal law will sometimes be relevant. This distinction between civil and criminal is reflected in the court structure and medical staff may need to attend both civil and criminal courts. One act may involve both civil and criminal liability: for example, if a member of staff hit a patient (or, more likely, a patient hit a member of staff!), this would be battery in civil law and an criminal assault under the Offences Against the Person Act 1861. Minor criminal matters such as assault will go to the magistrates' courts and more serious offences, such as manslaughter, will be dealt with at the Crown Court. A violent, unnatural or sudden death must be reported to the coroner, who may order a post mortem or hold an inquest. An inquest will take place in a coroner's court.

In civil law, negligence claims may be brought on the basis of a conditional fee agreement ('no win, no fee'). The lawyers for the winning side may claim a success fee of up to 100% for the case and this applies to all civil claims, including clinical negligence (formerly medical negligence), with the exception of family matters. Formerly, although the losing party did not need to pay their own lawyer, they did have to pay the other side's costs and take out an insurance policy to cover this. For medical negligence cases, the insurance premium could be thousands of pounds, which meant that many people would not take the risk of bringing a claim. Since 1 April 2000, under the

Conditional Fee Agreements Regulations 2000, the success fee and the insurance premium may be recovered from the other party under a costs order.

Lord Woolf's reforms of the civil justice system included the use of 'pre-action protocols'. The aim of the 'clinical negligence protocol' is to try to settle claims before they reach court. The claimant sends a 'preliminary notice' to the other side, setting out brief details and the value of the claim, and the other party must acknowledge this within 21 days. The parties may then decide to go through an alternative dispute resolution (ADR) procedure, under which they try to settle the claim. The next stage is a more detailed letter of claim, which must be acknowledged within 21 days. The parties should then conclude negotiations within six months. If the case should continue to court, then the procedure is set out in the Civil Procedure Rules 1998. These provide a common set of rules for both the County Court and the High Court. The court now takes an active part in the management of cases and also allocates each case to one of three 'tracks':

(a) the small claims track, which deals with claims under £5,000. Claims for personal injury must be no more than £1,000 to be allocated to this track. Parties cannot claim their legal costs from the other side;

(b) the fast track, which is for claims up to £15,000 where the trial is not expected to last for more than one day. Only one oral expert is allowed for each party;

(c) the multi-track, for claims over £15,000 and for complex cases. Most medical negligence claims will be multi-track claims and, if they are for over £50,000, will be heard in the High Court.

Claims in contract

Patients who suffer harm as a result of NHS treatment can sue for negligence. But can they sue for breach of contract? A patient receiving treatment from the NHS does not have a contract with the NHS and cannot sue for breach of contract if they suffer harm. Arguments have been put forward that a contract does exist. In *Pfizer v Ministry of Health* (1965), the House of Lords considered whether a patient paying for a prescription under the NHS was a contract. The House of Lords said that there was no contract between a patient and the NHS, even though a payment was made. A contract was marked out by the fact that it was a voluntary agreement, but pharmacists were under a statutory duty to provide the drugs required, so they did not do so voluntarily.

More recently, in *Reynolds v Health First Medical Group* (2000), the claimant consulted her GP (the defendants) in 1996 and was told that she was not pregnant, even though she was. When she realised that she was pregnant, it was too late to have an abortion. After having a baby, she claimed damages for pain and suffering, loss of earnings and the cost of bringing up the child. Although the original claim was made in negligence, the decision of *McFarlane v Tayside Health Board* (2000) (see below) prevented claims for bringing up the child in such circumstances and the claimant then claimed for breach of contract. This was based on the argument that a GP received a fee (capitation fee) for each patient on their list and, hence, consideration was provided. It was held by the county court that the fact that a GP received payment for each patient was not consideration. Even if it was consideration, there was still no contract because the relationship was controlled by statute (the National Health Service Act 1977) and there was no room for bargaining between the doctor and patient. Also, either the doctor or patient could end the relationship unilaterally, which could not be done in contracts.

If a patient paid for treatment at a private hospital and suffered harm as a result, they would have a claim for breach of contract. A patient suing in contract would have to show that the doctor did not reach the required standard of skill. At common law, the courts have said that the standard required is the same as that in negligence. In *Thake v Maurice* (1986), the Thakes had five children and did not want to have any more. Mr Thake paid a surgeon privately to carry out a vasectomy. The surgeon told Mr Thake that the operation was 'irreversible'. Later, Mrs Thake became pregnant but, not suspecting that she was, because of her husband's operation, she left it too late to have an abortion. The operation had been properly carried out but the effect had been reversed naturally. The Court of Appeal said that it was an implied term that the operation would be carried out with care and skill. Mr Thake argued that the surgeon had guaranteed that he would be sterile. The court held that the word 'irreversible' had to be interpreted in the context of medical science, where nothing could be guaranteed. It did not, therefore, mean irreversible, although it left open the possibility of a surgeon expressly guaranteeing a particular result. But the failure of the surgeon to give his usual warning about the risk of reversal was a breach of the duty of care in negligence and the claimants were entitled to damages for the distress suffered by

5

both of them and for the pain of birth. Patricia Thompson made a contract with Sheffield Fertility Clinic to provide IVF treatment and implant two embryos. The clinic implanted three and Patricia had triplets. She sued the clinic for breach of contract and won the case in the High Court ((2000) *The Independent*, 18 November).

It is now common practice for surgeons to warn of the risk of failure and this warning is contained in the consent form, which the patient will sign.

The Supply of Goods and Services Act (SGSA) 1982 is also important where a contract exists. If the contract simply consists of providing a service, for example, carrying out an operation to repair a hernia, then ss 13–15 of the SGSA 1982 apply. Section 13 provides that, where a service is provided in the course of a business, there is an implied term in the contract that it will be carried out with reasonable care and skill. Section 14 provides that, where a service is provided in the course of a business and the timescale cannot be determined from the contract, there is an implied term that it will be carried out within a reasonable time. Under s 15, where the price is not fixed by the contract, in a manner agreed in the contract or by a course of dealings, there is an implied term that a reasonable charge will be made.

If both goods and services are provided, for example, the fitting of a heart pacemaker, then, in addition to ss 13–15, ss 2–5 apply to the goods provided. Section 2 provides that there is an implied condition that the transferor has the right to transfer the property in the goods. If the sale is a sale by description, there is an implied condition that the goods will match the description (s 3). If the contract is made in the course of a business, there are implied conditions that the goods are of satisfactory quality unless any matter is brought to the buyer's attention or an examination ought to have revealed the defect. Also, there is an implied condition that the goods must be fit for their purpose (s 4). If the contract is made by sample, there is an implied condition that the goods will match the sample (s 5).

A patient suing for breach of contract will also have a claim in negligence.

Judicial review

The decisions of government and public bodies, which includes the NHS, are subject to judicial review. This means that the courts may examine the case to see whether the decision was made within the existing rules and in accordance with correct procedure. In considering the case, the courts will not look at the merits of a particular decision. The application is made to a Divisional Court of the Queen's Bench Division. The court may quash a decision, stop a body from exceeding its powers or order it to carry out a particular duty. The courts have refused to become involved in decisions about whether a particular patient should receive treatment. Section 3(1) of the National Health Service Act (NHSA) 1977 provides that it is the Secretary of State's duty to provide:

(a) hospital accommodation; ...

(e) such facilities for the prevention of illness, the care of persons suffering from illness and the aftercare of persons who have suffered from illness as he considers are appropriate as part of the health service;

(f) such other services as are required for the diagnosis and treatment of illness.

In *R v Secretary of State for Social Services ex p Hincks* (1979), patients complained that they had waited an unreasonable time for treatment because the hospital had postponed the building of a new block. They sought a declaration that the hospital was in breach of its duty under s 3(1) of the NHSA 1977. In rejecting the claim, it was held by the Court of Appeal that it was not the courts' function to say what funds should be given to the NHS and how to allocate them. Lord Denning said:

The Secretary of State says that he is doing the best he can with the financial resources available to him and I do not think that he can be faulted in the matter.

Other attempts to bring similar claims have all ended in failure. In *R v Central Birmingham HA ex p Walker* (1987), surgery on a baby was postponed five times because of a shortage of nurses. The Court of Appeal refused the application for judicial review and said that the health authority would have to make a decision that no reasonable body could have reached, that is, '*Wednesbury* unreasonableness'. This does not completely rule out a claim, but it would have to be an extreme decision by the health authority. In *R v Cambridge HA ex p B* (1995), the defendants refused to provide expensive treatment for a 10 year old girl with leukaemia, as they believed that it had less than a 10% chance of success. The Court of Appeal held that it was not part of the job of the courts to rule on the merits of medical decisions – they could only rule on the lawfulness of such decisions; here, the authority had acted lawfully.

More recently, in *R v Secretary of State for Health ex p Pfizer Ltd* (1999), the Secretary of State had issued a circular advising GPs not to prescribe Viagra for erectile dysfunction unless there were 'exceptional circumstances'. Pfizer sought judicial review, claiming that the circular prevented doctors from carrying out their statutory obligations. It was held that the advice overrode the professional judgment of doctors and, therefore, the circular was unlawful. Another recent claim for judicial review involved a refusal of treatment. In *R v North West Lancashire HA ex p A, D and G* (1999), the applicants suffered from transsexualism. They had been living as women and all wished to have gender reassignment surgery. Their health authority refused to refer them to a specialist clinic and refused to pay for the surgery. The policy of the health authority was that, although it considered transsexualism to be an illness, it only provided counselling in cases of 'overriding clinical need'. The court quashed the authority's decision to refuse treatment and the authority appealed. The Court of Appeal said that determining priorities was a matter of judgment for each authority and transsexualism would normally be lower down the scale than, say, kidney failure. But, as the authority accepted that transsexualism was an illness, its policies ought to reflect that. The only exception it considered was if transsexualism led to mental illness, so that anyone seeking treatment had to establish another illness. Effectively, the exception of 'overriding clinical need' was meaningless. The health authority's appeal was dismissed. The court also said that general recourse to the European Convention on Human Rights was unhelpful and cluttered the development of domestic legal principles. Claims for breach of Art 8 (respect for private and family life) for failure to protect sexual identity and breach of Art 3 (freedom from inhuman treatment) for failure to provide treatment were rejected.

The courts have made it clear that they cannot make judgments about the allocation of NHS resources, either in the case of individual patients or as regards types of treatment available. However, the mechanism of judicial review can bring wider benefits, in focusing attention on treatments which are short of funds, and may sometimes help the individual patient. In the case involving the girl with leukaemia, the treatment was paid for privately by a benefactor and this extended the girl's life.

The Human Rights Act 1998

The Human Rights Act (HRA) 1998 took effect from 2 October 2000. The Act effectively incorporates most of the European Convention on Human Rights into English law. All English courts have the right to deal with claims under the Convention. Schedule 1 to the HRA 1998 sets out the Articles from the Convention incorporated into the Act:

- Art 2   the right to life;

- Art 3   freedom from torture or degrading treatment;

- Art 4   freedom from slavery;

- Art 5   the right to liberty;

- Art 6   the right to a fair trial;

- Art 8   the right to respect for private and family life;

- Art 9   freedom of religion;

- Art 12   the right to marry and found a family;

- Art 14   freedom from discrimination.

Some rights are absolute and cannot be interfered with by the State in any circumstances – these are Arts 2, 3, 4 and 14. Other rights are subject to derogation (Arts 5 and 6). This means that the Government can apply restrictions to them; for example, Art 5, the right to liberty, is affected by legislation allowing suspected terrorists to be detained for seven days without appearing before a court. Other rights are qualified, for example, Arts 8 and 9, and these may be restricted in accordance with the law or if necessary for public safety or the protection of health and morals.

Under s 2 of the HRA 1998, courts dealing with Convention matters must take into account decisions of the European Court of Human Rights. The decisions are not binding but enable the law to move with changes in society. Under s 3, so far as it is possible to do so, primary and subordinate legislation must be read in such a way as to be compatible with the Convention. This means that, when interpreting legislation and statutory instruments, if the court is faced with a choice of interpretations, it must follow the one in keeping with the Convention. However, this is subject to the qualification, 'so far as it is possible to do so'. Under s 4, if a court determines that legislation is incompatible with the Convention, the High Court (and above) may make a 'declaration of incompatibility'. This does not make the legislation illegal but it is then open to Parliament to change the law. Under s 6, it is unlawful for a 'public authority' to act in a way which is incompatible with the Convention. A public authority is any body carrying out public functions and includes courts and tribunals. This would also include the Department of Health, health authorities, NHS Trusts and doctors acting in their NHS role. Presumably, it would also include a private hospital carrying out work for the NHS. Under s 7, anyone who suffers, or is likely to suffer, through a breach of the Convention may sue. Claims must be brought before the end of one year from the act complained of or such period as the court thinks equitable.

Some courts took the Human Rights Act 1998 into consideration before it came into force on 2 October 2000. In *C v North Devon HA ex p Coughlan* (1999), a disabled woman moved from a hospital into a purpose built NHS home after being told that it would be her home for life. Five years later, it was decided to close the home. The woman applied for judicial review of that decision. The Court of Appeal said that, first, moving the woman was unfair because it frustrated her legitimate expectation of a 'home for life' and there was no overriding public interest to justify the move; therefore, it was an abuse of power. Secondly, this was a breach of Art 8 of the European Convention on Human Rights (the right to respect for private and family life), because it interfered with her right to a home and could not be justified unless a suitable alternative was provided.

Probably the most important Articles for medical law will be Arts 2, 3, 5 and 8 (see Gordon, R and Ward, T, 'Human Rights Act: health law' (2000) 144(17) SJ 1). Under Art 2 (the right to life), there is a duty on the State to preserve life, although this is not an absolute duty. Article 3 (freedom from torture and degrading treatment) could be used for failure to provide treatment. Article 5 (the right to liberty) allows detention of people of unsound mind, but this must be according to law and must not be arbitrary. Article 8 (the right to private life) will be important in relation to confidentiality. Articles 6, 9, 12 and 14 may also be significant in enhancing patients' rights.

2 Consent to Treatment

You should be familiar with the following areas:

- the concept of capacity to consent
- if no consent: possible claims in trespass; assault and battery
- the requirements for a valid consent
- when a claim in negligence may arise from lack of information
- possible criminal offences: assaults under the OAPA 1861; gross negligence manslaughter; murder
- circumstances when treatment may be given without consent: necessity; best interests
- reform proposals

Introduction

The law of tort protects a person from being touched without their consent through the tort of trespass to the person. The law of consent reflects the ethical principle of autonomy, whereby the patient decides what should be done to their body. An act which amounts to trespass may also be a criminal offence, for which a person may be prosecuted. The tort of negligence might be relevant if the patient has not been given enough information before treatment. As a general rule, with medical treatment, the consent of the patient must be obtained before any treatment can be given, otherwise the patient has a right of action in trespass.

Capacity to consent

To be able to give a legally valid consent, the patient must have capacity to do so. Some people will clearly not have this capacity; for example, they may be unconscious, mentally handicapped, too young or unable to communicate. Others who do not fall into any of these categories may still be seen as lacking capacity, but the problem for the law is where to draw the line between those with and those without capacity. As a general rule, the patient must be able to understand the nature and purpose of the treatment to be able to consent to it. Medical staff have to make the decision in individual cases whether that particular patient has the capacity to consent to that particular treatment. A number of factors will be relevant, including the nature of the treatment, whether the patient has been taking medication, etc. The Law Commission has recommended that capacity to make decisions should be assessed on the 'balance of probabilities' (*Mental Incapacity*, Law Com 231, 1995).

A number of cases have given guidance on determining a patient's capacity. In *Re T (Adult: Refusal of Treatment)* (1992), T, a pregnant woman, was involved in a car accident. If she was not given a blood transfusion, she would die. T was not a Jehovah's Witness, although her mother was. After the mother spoke to T, T refused a transfusion. The Court of Appeal held that the hospital could ignore T's refusal, as T did not have the capacity to consent because of the undue influence of her mother.

However, in the following case, the courts accepted the importance of the patient's beliefs. In *Re C (Adult: Refusal of Treatment)* (1994), C, who suffered from paranoid schizophrenia and had delusions that he was a doctor, was detained in Broadmoor Hospital. He developed gangrene in his foot and the doctor said that amputation at the knee was necessary to save his life, but C refused this. Other treatment was successful but C wanted a declaration from the court that no amputation should be done without his consent. The court had to consider whether C had capacity and used the test of whether he understood the nature, purpose and effect of medical treatment. The court said that he *did* understand the information he had been given and that he had made a clear choice.

In *Re MB (Medical Treatment)* (1997), the Court of Appeal approved *Re C* in a case where a woman who was 40 weeks pregnant was admitted to hospital with the foetus in the breach position. Normal delivery would put both the woman's life and that of the baby in danger. She agreed to a Caesarean operation but refused at the last minute because of a fear of needles. The court held that a patient lacked capacity if: (a) the patient is unable to understand and retain information needed to make a decision; and (b) the patient cannot use information and weigh it in the balance, for example, if they suffer from a phobia. The court said that the patient temporarily lacked capacity because of her phobia, and it authorised the operation.

In *St George's Healthcare NHS Trust v S* (1998), the Court of Appeal laid down guidelines for dealing with patients who were believed to lack capacity. These are as follows:

- the guidelines do not apply if the patient is competent;

- if a competent patient refuses consent, application to the High Court is pointless. The hospital should make a written record of the patient's decision;

- if the patient is incapable of giving or refusing consent, the authority can act in the best interests of the patient. If there is an advance directive, that should normally be followed;

- the authority should identify as soon as possible if there is concern over competence;

- the patient's family doctor may be qualified to make the assessment, but, in difficult cases about future health or the life of the patient, an independent psychiatrist should assess the patient. If there is still serious doubt about competence, the court should be involved;

- if the patient is unable or incapable of instructing solicitors, the Official Solicitor should be notified.

The guidelines then deal with the hearing of the matter, saying that both parties should be involved.

In response to the Law Commission's Report on *Mental Incapacity*, the Government, in *Making Decisions* (Cm 4465, 1999), proposed a new test of capacity, based on the Law Commission's functional approach. This would focus on whether the individual is able to understand the nature and effect of the decision at the time that a particular decision is made (para 1.4). The following definitions of incapacity will be incorporated in legislation:

- A person is without capacity if, at the time that a decision needs to be taken, he or she is unable by reason of mental disability to make a decision on the matter in question; or unable to communicate a decision on that matter because he or she is unconscious; or for any other reason.

13

- Mental disability is any disability or disorder of the mind or brain, whether permanent or temporary, which results in an impairment or disturbance of mental functioning.

- A person is to be regarded as unable to make a decision by reason of mental disability if the disability is such that, at the time when the decision needs to be made, the person is unable to understand or retain the information relevant to the decision, or unable to make a decision based on that information.

Civil law

The tort of trespass to the person consists of assault, battery and false imprisonment. False imprisonment involves restricting a person's freedom of movement and it is much less likely to occur in medical treatment than assault and battery. However, in the *St George's* case, the patient was detained against her will and given a Caesarean section, so a claim could have been made for false imprisonment.

An assault is an act which causes someone to apprehend unlawful force against them, for example, a doctor holding a needle who approaches a patient, intending to give them an injection without their consent.

A battery is the infliction of unlawful force on another, for example, an actual injection given without consent. It has long been accepted that touching someone without consent is a battery. In *Scholendorff v Society of New York Hospital* (1914), Cardozo J stated:

> Every human being of adult years and sound mind has a right to determine what shall be done with his own body; and a surgeon who performs an operation without the patient's consent commits an assault.

Trespass to the person is an intentional tort, which means that the act, rather than the injury, is intended. This type of tort is in contrast to an unintentional tort, such as negligence, where the act is not intended. With intentional torts, legal action may be taken without proving actual damage: it is enough to prove that the act took place. Consequently, a patient may sue for battery even though they have not suffered any injury. With unintentional torts, actual damage must be proved.

Consent by the patient may be expressly given or may be implied. An example of express consent is where the patient agrees to a proposed operation. Consent may be implied by a patient holding out a cut hand. It is standard practice to ask a patient to sign a consent form before an operation. However, it is important to realise that merely signing such a form, without an explanation of the treatment and agreement to the treatment, would not be a valid consent. Clearly, if the patient agrees to a particular operation and the doctor carries out a different one in error, that is trespass.

In order for a patient to give a valid consent to treatment, the patient must know what the proposed treatment is. But the question arises of how much information the patient must be given. In the US, the concept of 'informed' consent requires that the patient must be given sufficient facts about the proposed treatment to give a proper consent. This concept has not been followed by the English courts. What must be disclosed to obtain a valid consent in English law? In *Chatterton v Gerson* (1981), C suffered pain from a scar following a hernia operation. G, a surgeon, proposed an injection near the spinal cord. Following this, C lost all sensation in her right leg and argued that, as she had not been given sufficient information about the risks, she could not give a valid consent. The court held that, where the patient is told in 'broad terms' about the nature of the procedure, that is sufficient. C's claim for battery failed, as she knew the general nature of the treatment. The court also said that, if the nature of the operation has been explained but the risks have not, then any claim should be in negligence, rather than trespass.

The application of the test from *Chatterton v Gerson* is not always straightforward. If a patient consents to a blood test but is not told that the test includes testing for HIV, has the patient consented?

Consent and negligence

To establish negligence in a medical context, it has to be shown that the doctor owes the patient a duty of care, that the doctor has broken this duty and that the patient has suffered damage as a result, that is, that the breach caused the loss (*Donoghue v Stevenson* (1932)). The doctor's duty of care in negligence includes a duty to give sufficient advice to enable the patient to make a rational decision about treatment. A patient who brings a claim for negligence on the basis of lack of information has to show that this breach caused the loss. To establish this, the patient would have to prove that, if they had been given the extra information, they would not have consented to the procedure. Whether a doctor has acted negligently is not judged by the normal negligence standard of the 'reasonable man', but by the *Bolam* test. This provides that, if a doctor (or other health worker) reaches the standard of 'a responsible body of medical opinion' (*Bolam v Friern HMC* (1957), *per* McNair J), they are not negligent. If a patient is claiming that they have not been given sufficient information about the risks, their claim should be in negligence. In *Chatterton v Gerson* (1981), Bristow J stated:

> In my judgment, once the patient is informed in broad terms of the nature of the procedure which is intended and gives her consent, that consent is real and the cause of the action on which to base a claim for failure to go into risks and implications is negligence, not trespass.

In the US, the courts have adopted the 'prudent patient' test. This test uses the standard of a reasonable person in the patient's position – would they see the risks as an important factor in deciding whether or not to have treatment?

In Canada, the courts have said that a patient has the right to know about the risks (*Reibl v Hughes* (1980)). This has been qualified to the extent that a patient may waive this 'right to know', by giving the doctor the right to make the decision.

The question of whether the *Bolam* test applied to information about risks as well as to diagnosis and medical treatment was determined in *Sidaway v Governors of Bethlem Royal Hospital* (1985). After an accident at work, S had pain in her shoulder. Dr F diagnosed pressure on a nerve root and S consented to an operation, as a result of which she became paralysed. S claimed that she had not been told about a 2% risk to a nerve root and a 1% risk of damage to her spinal cord. It was found that she had been told of the damage to the nerve root. S claimed that failure to warn of the damage to the spinal cord meant that her consent was invalid and the doctor was liable in battery. S also claimed that not telling her of the risk was negligence. It was held by the House of Lords that, if S understood the general nature of the operation, not being told of the risks did not mean that it was battery. As regards her negligence claim, in warning of risks, if the doctor conformed to a responsible body of medical opinion as to what to tell the patient, the doctor had fulfilled this duty. It was found that the doctor in this case had done so. Also, the patient understood the nature of the operation, so both claims failed. In the House of Lords, Lord Scarman argued in favour of the prudent patient test, rather than the *Bolam* test.

The House of Lords also confirmed that a doctor could withhold information from a patient on the ground of 'therapeutic privilege', if the doctor considered that the information would be detrimental to the health of that patient.

If a patient asks the doctor questions about the risks, does the doctor have to answer? In the Australian case of *Rogers v Whitaker* (1992), R, who was blind in her right eye, was advised to have an operation on that eye to restore sight to it. She asked many questions about the operation but was not told of a one in 14,000 chance of going blind in her left eye as a result of the operation. The operation was carried out without negligence but she went blind in her left eye. It was held by the High Court, which refused to follow *Bolam*, that, as a matter of general principle, the doctor had been negligent in not telling R of this risk. It did not matter that the patient had not asked about that particular risk. In the UK, however, the courts follow the *Bolam* test of whether a responsible body of medical opinion would answer such questions. If there was a duty to answer specific questions, a knowledgeable and articulate patient would have an advantage over others.

Non-therapeutic treatment

Non-therapeutic treatment is not given to make the patient better but for some other reason. Examples would include cosmetic surgery and treatment for contraceptive purposes. This is in contrast to therapeutic treatment, which is needed because the patient is suffering from an illness. Are the rules on consent different for non-therapeutic treatment? In *Gold v Haringay HA* (1987), Mrs G consented to be sterilised but was not told of the risk of natural reversal. When she became pregnant, she sued for negligence, claiming that she had not been told of the risks or alternatives. It was held in the High Court that, in non-therapeutic cases, the duty of care demands that the patient should be given all the information that a reasonable patient would want to know. The Court of Appeal overruled this decision and said that giving treatment or advice involved professional skill and the *Bolam* test applied. The court also said that the distinction between therapeutic and non-therapeutic treatment was often difficult to make and should not be made the basis for different standards of care. Some doctors did warn of the risk of reversal and others did not; therefore, Mrs G's claim failed.

Criminal law

It is possible for medical staff to be charged with criminal offences arising out of their work. These offences range from minor criminal assaults to grievous bodily harm and, finally, manslaughter or murder. In all criminal offences, the prosecution have to prove both that the defendant had *mens rea* (the intention to commit the act) and that he had committed the *actus reus* (the actual act).

As in civil law, a criminal assault at common law is a threat of violence and battery involves some physical contact. Statute, in the form of the Offences Against the Person Act (OAPA) 1861, also provides a number of offences. Under s 47 of the OAPA 1861, an 'assault occasioning actual bodily harm' is an offence. If a patient is given treatment without their consent or is given treatment in spite of their refusing to give consent, then medical staff could face prosecution. Treatment such as cauterising a blood vessel would fall within this section.

Section 18 of the OAPA 1861 provides that it is an offence to unlawfully and maliciously wound or cause any grievous bodily harm with intent to do grievous bodily harm. This is the most serious offence involving assault and includes both wounding, where the skin is broken (*C v Eisenhower* (1983)), and serious harm (grievous bodily harm). The distinguishing factor from s 20 (see below) is that there must be a specific intent. If medical staff carry out a surgical procedure without consent, they could be charged under this section. A failure to treat, leading to serious harm, might also be regarded as 'causing' that harm and could lead to prosecution.

Under s 20 of the OAPA 1861, it is an offence to 'unlawfully and maliciously wound or inflict any grievous bodily harm upon any person, either with or without any weapon or instrument'. Under this section, the damage must be inflicted, rather than caused, as under s 18. If medical staff fail to treat a patient, resulting in serious harm, they cannot be convicted under s 20, as they have not inflicted harm on the patient.

In all of the above offences, if the patient consents to the treatment, this will provide a valid defence. However, this must be qualified, to the extent that there are certain things which a person cannot consent to. For example, could a patient give a valid consent to having their arm amputated if there was nothing wrong with it? In *R v Brown* (1992), the court said that consent was not a defence to acts which caused actual bodily harm or wounding. Consequently, a patient could not give a valid consent to a medical procedure which was not medically necessary and which caused harm to the patient. A valid consent could be given to a procedure which involved harm but was medically needed, for example, amputation of a limb to stop the spread of gangrene.

It would be rare for medical staff to face a prosecution for murder or manslaughter, although this is not unknown, as shown by the cases of the nurse Beverly Allitt and the prosecution in 1999 of the GP Dr Harold Shipman. Murder is a common law offence, which requires the prosecution to prove the intention to kill or cause serious harm and the relevant act causing death. In *R v Cox* (1992), Dr Cox was charged with murder after he gave an elderly patient, who was in great pain, an injection of potassium chloride (which has no therapeutic value). The patient died within minutes but the doctor was only convicted of attempted murder, because it could not be proved that he gave the injection with the intention of killing the patient rather than simply to ease her pain.

Manslaughter is divided into voluntary manslaughter, which falls under the Homicide Act 1957, and involuntary manslaughter. The latter is divided into unlawful act manslaughter and gross negligence manslaughter. Gross negligence manslaughter involves carrying out a lawful act but in a reckless way. In *R v Adomako* (1995), the defendant anaesthetist failed to notice that an oxygen tube had been disconnected for several minutes, as a result of which the patient died. It was held that the defendant owed a duty of care to the patient, that he had been grossly negligent and that the patient died as a result. The defendant was convicted of manslaughter. In this case, the negligence consisted of an omission to act.

Treating without consent

To be able to give a legally valid consent to treatment, the patient must be recognised as competent to do so by the law. An adult patient is regarded as being able to consent to treatment unless there is evidence to show otherwise. However, in some circumstances, a person may not be competent to give consent – for example, those suffering from mental impairment or from a physical injury which prevents them from giving consent. Children under 16 are not treated by the law as having competence to consent (see below, Chapter 3).

The law regards anyone who reaches the age of 18 and who is mentally competent as an adult (Family Law Reform Act 1969). In the case of medical treatment, a child of 16 years who is mentally competent can consent to treatment.

When someone reaches the age of 18, no one else may consent for them, but, if the patient is over 18 and is mentally incompetent, this creates a problem. This situation has been described as a 'legal limbo' by Margaret Brazier (*Medicine, Patients and the Law*, 1992, Penguin), because the patient cannot consent and no one may consent on their behalf.

In some circumstances, treatment may be given without consent. At common law, treatment may be given on the basis of the doctrine of necessity, or acting in the patient's 'best interests'. Children can be made wards of court and this enables the court to make decisions about their treatment, but the same cannot be done with adults. A number of statutes also provide that treatment may be given without the consent of the patient. If a patient is compulsorily detained under the Mental Health Act 1983, they may be given treatment for their mental condition without their consent. The Public Health (Control of Disease) Act 1984 provides that those suffering from certain notifiable diseases, such as cholera, may be given a compulsory examination without their consent and may be detained in hospital.

If a patient suffers from mental incapacity but has not been compulsorily detained, the problem of consent remains. In *F v West Berkshire HA* (1989), F was 36 years old but had a mental age of five. She was a voluntary patient in a mental hospital. She began a sexual relationship with another patient and, as she would be unable to look after any child which might be born, the question arose as to whether F could be sterilised. Clearly, F was unable to give a valid consent to such a procedure. A declaration was sought as to the legality of sterilisation. The House of Lords confirmed that, if an adult patient could not give consent because they were unconscious or suffered from mental disability, a doctor could provide treatment on the basis of the principle of necessity only if it would save their life, improve their health or prevent a deterioration in their health. A declaration was granted that F could lawfully be sterilised. The court said that, if the proposed treatment was radical or irreversible, the doctor should apply to the court for a declaration.

It may often be difficult for doctors to judge whether an adult has the capacity to consent. In *St George's Healthcare NHS Trust v S* (1998), S was a 36 year old pregnant woman who was diagnosed with preeclampsia and advised that she should go to hospital for an induced birth. S wanted a natural birth and refused to go into hospital. S was then seen by a social worker and two doctors and was compulsorily admitted under the Mental Health Act 1983. The hospital obtained a declaration from the court which enabled them to act without S's consent and they carried out a Caesarean operation. S then appealed to the Court of Appeal, which said that a competent pregnant woman has the right to refuse treatment, even if refusing put her life in danger, and the hospital had committed trespass. The court criticised the use of the Mental Health Act to detain a patient who simply had different views from the majority.

The principle of necessity

In order for the principle of necessity to operate, two requirements must be met: (a) there must be a necessity to act in a situation where medical staff cannot communicate with the patient; and (b) the action taken must be what a reasonable person would do in the best interests of the patient (*Re F Mental Patient: Sterilisation* (1990), *per* Lord Goff). Guidance on how this principle works can be found in two Canadian cases. In *Marshall v Curry* (1933), during an operation to repair a hernia, the patient was found to have a diseased testicle. The doctor believed that the testicle was a danger to the patient's life and removed it. When the patient found out, he sued for battery. The court held that, in an emergency, a doctor may act without the patient's consent to save their life or preserve their health. In the circumstances, this was not a battery. In *Murray v McMurchy* (1949), during a Caesarean operation, it was found that tumours in the patient's uterus would have made it dangerous for her if she became pregnant again. The doctor tied her fallopian tubes to prevent a future pregnancy. The court held that there was no evidence that the tumours were an immediate danger to her life or health. The doctor was liable for battery. The doctor could quite easily have waited and obtained the consent of the patient.

These cases illustrate that a distinction can be made between doing an act which is a necessity and doing something which is simply convenient. In the English case of *Devi v West Midlands RHA* (1981), the patient had consented to repair of her uterus and the surgeon also performed a sterilisation operation, which he believed was in her best interests. It was held that the surgeon was liable in battery.

21

The best interests of the patient

Another basis on which a doctor may treat a patient without their consent is if the doctor acts in the best interests of the patient. This raises the question of who decides what is in the best interests of the patient. The answer to this is that the *Bolam* test applies – what a responsible body of medical opinion would say was in the best interests of the patient. In *F v West Berkshire HA* (1989), the House of Lords confirmed that the *Bolam* test applied when determining the best interests of a patient who could not consent. Neill LJ had argued in the Court of Appeal that the test should be that it was 'unreasonable, in the opinion of most experts in the field', not to carry out the operation. This test is stricter than *Bolam*, which merely requires a group of doctors who would agree to carry out such an operation.

Although *F v West Berkshire HA* effectively decided that doctors make the decision of what is in the best interests of the patient, it still left open the question of what exactly is in the patient's 'best interests'. What is in the patient's best interests is not simply a matter of clinical judgment by doctors, but may include the patient's beliefs and way of life. The Court of Appeal has recently qualified the approach to be taken in two cases. In *R-B (A Patient) v Official Solicitor* (2000), the Court of Appeal considered the case of A, a 28 year old man with Down's syndrome, who lived with his mother and attended a day centre. The mother was not in good health and was concerned that, if A went into local authority care, he may have sexual relations with another patient and make them pregnant. A could not understand the link between sex and pregnancy and, although he had said that he did not want to be sterilised, he could not validly consent or refuse. His mother applied to the High Court to exercise its inherent jurisdiction to allow A to be sterilised in his best interests but the court refused the application, saying that a vasectomy was not essential for A's well being.

On appeal, the Court of Appeal applied *Re F (Mental Patient: Sterilisation)* (1990) and said that, as regards the sterilisation of an adult who was unable to consent, it had to be shown that the procedure was in their best interests. The court said that 'best interests' included medical, emotional and other welfare issues. Doctors making decisions about best interests had a duty to act in accordance with a responsible body of medical opinion. But there was also a second duty – to act in the best interests of the mentally incapacitated patient. In such applications, it was the judge, not the doctor, who decided whether the operation was in the best interests of the patient. In applying these principles, the court said that sterilisation would not give A more freedom, save him from exploitation or help him to deal with the emotional implications of a close relationship; the operation was not in his best interests. The court emphasised that the interests of the patient were paramount but left open the question of whether third party interests should be considered.

In *Re S* (2000), S was a 29 year old woman who had severe learning difficulties and lived with her mother. She was moving into a local authority home and her mother was worried that S may become pregnant. The choice was either to have a hysterectomy or to have a coil fitted, and both procedures would effectively sterilise S. The judge at first instance said that it was for the mother to decide. The Court of Appeal said that, once a court decided that the proposed treatment was within the range covered by the *Bolam* test, that test then became irrelevant to the decision of what was in the 'best interests' of the patient. It was for the court to decide this, taking into account broader ethical, social and moral considerations than those in *Bolam*. The court said that a disabled patient had the right not to have drastic surgery imposed unless this was in their best interests; here, the less invasive treatment was best.

Should relatives be consulted about the best interests of the patient? Although relatives are often asked in practice, they have no legal right to consent to treatment for adult patients. However, see the proposals for reform, below.

Reform of the law on mental incapacity

The Law Commission examined the law in this area in *Mental Incapacity* (Law Com 231, 1995) and made a number of proposals:

- there should be a presumption against lack of capacity;

- any decisions made on behalf of someone without capacity should be made in their best interests (as there is no other viable alternative). In the draft Mental Incapacity Bill, cl 3 sets out the proposed test of 'best interests':

  ... in deciding what is in a person's best interests, regard shall be had to the following:

  (a) so far as ascertainable, his past and present wishes and feelings and the factors which he would consider if he were able to do so;

    (b) the need to permit and encourage that person to participate, or to improve his ability to participate, as fully as possible in anything done for and any decision affecting him;

    (c) if it is practicable and appropriate to consult them, the views as to that person's wishes and feelings and as to what would be in his best interests of:

        (i) any person named by him as someone to be consulted on those matters;

        (ii) anyone [whether his spouse, a relative, friend or other person] engaged in caring for him or interested in his welfare;

        (iii) the donee of any continuing power of attorney granted by him;

        (iv) any manager appointed for him by the court;

    (d) whether the purpose for which any action or decision is required can be as effectively achieved in a manner less restrictive of his freedom of action;

- there should be a general authority to act reasonably for the personal welfare or healthcare of a person without capacity.

The Report made a number of other proposals, including the following: 'advance refusals of treatment' (advance directives) should be respected when the patient later lacks capacity; certain treatments, such as sterilisation and organ donation, would need permission of the court; and there should be a new power – a 'continuing power of attorney' – which would give the donee of that power the right to make decisions for a donor who lacks capacity. This power should cover the donor's personal welfare, healthcare, property and affairs.

The Government's response included a Consultation Paper (*Who Decides? Making Decisions on Behalf of Mentally Incapacitated Adults*, 1997) and a Report, *Making Decisions* (Cm 4465, 1999). The Government proposals in *Making Decisions* would apply to those people aged 16 or over who lack capacity. The Government accepted most of the proposals, including the three main points listed above. However, it did not accept the proposals for advance directives. The Report stated:

> The Government believes that a clear statement of the present legal position concerning advance statements would be helpful to lawyers, doctors and patients [Chapter 1, para 16].

But it added:

> Given the division of opinion which exists on this complex subject, and given the flexibility inherent in developing case law, the Government believes that it would not be appropriate to legislate at the present time and thus fix the statutory position once and for all [Chapter 1, para 20].

Some of the main proposals are set out below:

- Capacity: there will be a presumption against lack of capacity. This means that it is presumed that someone can make decisions, unless it is proven otherwise. There will be a 'functional approach' to determining capacity, that is, can the person make that particular decision at the time? A new statutory definition of incapacity is based on the fact that someone is 'unable by reason of mental disability to make a decision' on the particular matter in question, or unable to communicate a decision because he or she is unconscious. Also, all practical steps must be taken to enable someone without capacity to communicate their decisions.

- Best interests: decisions made on behalf of people without capacity must be made in their best interests. The factors suggested in the Law Commission's draft Bill were accepted.

- General authority to act reasonably: there should be a general authority to act reasonably for the personal welfare or healthcare of someone lacking capacity. This was proposed by the Law Commission. Such a general authority would help those making day to day decisions for people who lack capacity. The present law protects neither the person without capacity nor the carer. The general authority will not cover some decisions which no one may make on behalf of someone lacking capacity. These decisions include consent to marriage, consent to sexual relations, consent to divorce, consent to adoption and voting at elections.

- Continuing power of attorney: proposals to introduce this new power were accepted. It will replace the existing system of enduring power of attorney, which only covers financial matters. The new power would cover financial, personal welfare and healthcare matters.

- Court of Protection: there should be a new court (whose name is to be decided) to replace the existing Court of Protection. The new court would be able to make decisions on behalf of those lacking capacity. The new court should have regional centres and not simply be based in London, like the existing Court of Protection.

The law on incapacity has been in need of reform for several years and these proposals should eliminate many of the existing problems.

Codes of Practice

In 1999, the General Medical Council issued guidance for doctors in *Seeking Patients' Consent: The Ethical Considerations*. This sets out in detail how doctors should approach obtaining consent and, amongst other things, covers the following matters: providing sufficient information for patients; obtaining consent with adults; the mentally incompetent; children; dealing with questions; advance statements; and when to apply to the court.

The Human Rights Act 1998

Article 3 (the right not to be subjected to degrading treatment) could be used in situations like *S v St George's NHS Trust* (1998), where S was forced to have a Caesarean section against her will. It could also be used by an anorexic patient who was fed against his or her wishes. Article 8 (respect for private life) covers physical integrity and could be used if a patient is given treatment without consent. Article 9 (freedom of religion) may be relied upon if someone's religious beliefs are ignored and they are given treatment, for example, Jehovah's Witnesses who are given a blood transfusion.

3 Children and Consent

You should be familiar with the following areas:

- capacity to consent: children over 16 years; *Gillick* competence
- competent children; young children
- effect of refusal of consent: by minors; by parents
- limits on parents' powers
- refusal by both children and parents

Introduction

This chapter will examine the circumstances where children are competent to consent to treatment and where parents may consent on behalf of children, and the problems which arise when there is a conflict between the views of parents and children. The area of refusal of treatment causes difficulties for the law, particularly in determining the extent to which children may refuse treatment where that refusal may result in serious injury or death. Applications may be made to the court under s 8 of the Children Act 1989 for a specific issue order; or the child (if under 18) may be made a ward of court; or the court may use its inherent power under its *parens patriae* jurisdiction to make decisions for a child.

Consent not needed

Treatment may be given without consent under the principle of necessity, for example, in an emergency. Also, if a child has been abandoned by their parents, treatment may be given without consent.

Capacity to consent

A child, or minor, is someone under the age of 18. It is important for medical staff to obtain consent before treating a child for the same reasons as for adult patients: it would otherwise be trespass to the person. The question arises of when a child is competent to consent to medical treatment. Section 8(1) of the Family Law Reform Act 1969 provides:

> The consent of a minor who has attained the age of 16 years to any surgical, medical or dental treatment which, in the absence of consent, would constitute a trespass to the person ... shall be effective as it would be if he were of full age.

A child aged 16 can, therefore, consent to treatment. A parent cannot override a consent by the child. But s 8 does not cover the child donating blood or an organ.

What about children under 16?

The common law has developed rules for such children. The leading case is *Gillick v West Norfolk and Wisbech AHA* (1985). The Department of Health and Social Security (DHSS) issued guidance to doctors, stating that they could give contraceptive advice and treatment to girls under 16. They could do this without the consent of the parents, if the child did not want the parents to be involved. Mrs Gillick, who had several daughters under 16, sought a declaration that it was unlawful to treat children under 16 without their parents' consent. The House of Lords held by a majority of 3:2 that this advice by the DHSS was not unlawful. They said that a child under 16 could give a valid consent to medical treatment in certain circumstances without their parents' consent. Lord Scarman said that the parents' right to consent for their child who is under 16 yields to the child's right when he reaches 'a sufficient understanding and intelligence' to be able to make up his own mind. Lord Fraser said that the doctor could give contraceptive advice and treatment but must be satisfied about five matters:

(a) the girl will understand the advice;

(b) the doctor cannot persuade her to tell her parents;

(c) she is likely to begin having sex, or continue to have sex, without contraception;

(d) unless she receives advice/treatment, her health will suffer;

(e) it is in her best interests to receive advice/treatment.

This case laid down the test for determining whether a child under 16 could consent to medical treatment, and it became known as the 'Gillick test', or the test of 'Gillick competence'. Although the test can work for many treatments, the boundaries of the test are not clear. For example, a 15 year old may consent to having their tonsils removed, a 10 year old may consent to treatment for minor cuts and bruises and a 'Gillick competent' child can consent to giving blood. But could a child under 18 consent to donating a kidney? Although this seems unlikely, there are cases in between these examples which are not clear.

As regards young children who are not Gillick competent, their parents may give a legally valid consent for them. Margaret Brazier, in Medicine, Patients and the Law (1992, Penguin), considers that children under 12 virtually never have the maturity to consent to treatment. The parents' right to consent is limited, in that it must be exercised in the 'best interests' of the child.

If a parent refuses to allow a child to have any medical treatment when they need it, this would amount to neglect causing injury to health under s 1 of the Children and Young Persons Act 1933, which is a criminal offence.

Refusal of consent

(a) By a minor

If a child refuses to consent to treatment, can anyone consent for the child? Although the Family Law Reform Act 1969 gave children aged 16 the right to consent to treatment, it did not deal with the power to refuse treatment. What is the position of the Gillick competent child – can they refuse treatment? The matter was dealt with in R (A Minor) (Wardship: Medical Treatment) (1991). R was a 15 year old girl who was placed in a children's home after a fight with her father. Her mental state deteriorated and she attacked her father with a hammer. She was then placed in a psychiatric unit, where doctors wanted to give her anti-psychotic drugs, but she refused. The local authority made her a ward of court, so as to obtain the court's permission to give her the drugs without her consent. The court considered Lord Scarman's speech in *Gillick* and said that the parents' right to consent does not end when the child becomes *Gillick* competent. Lord Donaldson made an analogy between having the power to give consent and having the key to a door. The child can obtain this 'key' by reaching 16 years or by becoming *Gillick* competent; but the parents also have keys and they can give consent even if a competent child refuses. On the facts, even though R had periods of lucidity, she was incompetent and the court authorised the doctors to give her medication.

A doctor who is faced with a child who refuses treatment may obtain a consent to treatment from a parent. The Court of Appeal again considered the matter in *Re W (A Minor) (Medical Treatment)* (1992). W, a 16 year old girl who had anorexia, was taken into a residential home but her condition worsened and doctors wished to move her to a special hospital. W refused to consent to the move. The local authority applied to the court under the Children Act 1989 for a declaration that it would be lawful to move her. The Court of Appeal held that, although W was *Gillick* competent, the court had an inherent power to make the order. The nature of the illness was such that patients did not wish to be cured. Lord Donaldson said that his 'keyholder' analogy was wrong, because keys could lock doors but a child could not refuse treatment. Instead, he drew an analogy with a 'flakjacket'. A valid consent acted like a flakjacket for a doctor and provided a defence to a claim in trespass. The flakjacket could be provided by a competent child or a parent. The right of a 16 year old to consent cannot be overridden by a parent but this can be done by the court; and the right of a *Gillick* competent child to consent cannot be overridden by a parent but can be overridden by the court. But, if any child under 18 refuses treatment, consent may be given by a parent or the court. Lord Donaldson said:

> No minor, of whatever age, has power, by refusing consent to treatment, to override a consent to treatment by someone who has parental responsibility for the minor and, *a fortiori*, a consent by the court.

A number of commentators have argued that the power to refuse treatment is the corollary of the power to consent to treatment and, logically, someone who can consent should be able to refuse. But Mason and McCall-Smith (*Law and Medical Ethics*, 5th edn, 1999, Butterworths) point out that a distinction can be made between consent and refusal. Consent is an acceptance of the view of an experienced doctor, while refusal is rejecting this experience. The consequences of the latter may be far more serious.

The court did accept in *Re W* that, in making a decision, the fact that the minor refused treatment would be taken into account.

The power of the court to overrule a minor's refusal of treatment stems from its *parens patriae* jurisdiction. This means 'parent of the country' and formed part of the prerogative powers of the Crown to look after those citizens who needed protection. The court will look to see whether the minor has the capacity to refuse treatment and, if this is not established, it will authorise treatment, as in *Re R* (1991) and *Re W (A Minor)* (1992), above. In exercising its powers, the court will act in the best interests of the child.

(b) By a parent

What if the parents refuse to consent to medical treatment for their child? If the child is over 16 or is *Gillick* competent, then the child may consent to treatment. But if the child is too young or too immature and cannot give a valid consent, what is the legal position of the doctor as regards giving treatment?

The classic example is a critically ill baby whose parents refuse to consent to treatment because of their own religious beliefs. In *Re R (A Minor) (Blood Transfusion)* (1993), R was a 10 month old girl with leukaemia who needed blood transfusions. Her parents, who were Jehovah's Witnesses, refused to consent. The local authority applied under s 8 of the Children Act 1989 for a specific issue order to allow the transfusions to be given. The court said that the main consideration was the welfare of the child. The child was too young to express her wishes and, without treatment, she would suffer harm. The court could override the parents, as it was in the child's best interests.

But this type of decision is not an easy one for the court to make, because it must consider the effect on the child if the court goes against the wishes of the parents. The child could, for example, be rejected by the religious community. The circumstances of the case are also important, whether it is an emergency or whether there is time to refer it to court for a considered decision. The court must balance the various factors, including the religious beliefs of the parents. In *Re S (A Minor)* (1993), S was a four year old boy with leukaemia who needed treatment, including a blood transfusion. His parents were Jehovah's Witnesses and refused to allow him to undergo a transfusion. The local authority asked the court for an order under the court's inherent jurisdiction. The court took into account the fact that the treatment would give the boy a 50% chance of living and granted the order allowing treatment. As regards the argument that the child would suffer rejection, the court said that *it* had made the decision and, thus, the parents were absolved of blame.

More recently, in *Re C (A Child) (HIV Testing)* (1999), the parents refused to have their child tested for HIV, although her mother was HIV positive. Both parents opposed the traditional method of treating the disease and believed that it would not be to C's benefit. When the baby was five months old, the doctors believed that it would be in the child's best interests to be tested, as knowledge of her HIV status was important in determining future treatment. If the child was found to be free of the disease, doctors would then recommend that breast feeding should stop, which would further improve the child's chances of avoiding the disease. An application was made for a specific issue order under the Children Act 1989 that C be tested, and the Official Solicitor acted as the child's guardian *ad litem*. At first instance, an order was granted but an application for leave to appeal was made by the parents. The Court of Appeal said that a court could overrule the decision of a reasonable parent and, on the scientific evidence, the case for testing was overwhelming. Leave to appeal was refused.

In *Re A (Children)* (2000), the Court of Appeal had to consider the very difficult case of the conjoined Siamese twins, Jodie and Mary. Jodie had the potential to lead a separate, independent existence but Mary's heart and lungs did not function properly and she was dependent on Jodie for oxygenated blood. If an operation to separate them was not carried out, they would die within three to six months because Jodie's heart would fail. The parents were Roman Catholics and they refused to consent to the operation, as they believed that both twins had a right to life. The doctors wanted to carry out an operation to separate the twins because they believed that Jodie could have a worthwhile life, although Mary would inevitably die. An application was made by the NHS Trust under the inherent jurisdiction of the court. The leading judgment was given by Ward LJ. Such an operation could not be in Mary's best interests because it took away her right to life but it was in Jodie's best interests. In resolving this conflict, the court had to choose the lesser of two evils. It also had to consider the wishes of the parents, which should be given great respect; however, their wishes were not in the children's best interests. The best interests of the twins was to give the chance of life to the one who could benefit from it, even if to do that was to end the life of the other twin. The other important question to decide was whether the proposed operation was lawful, as it would involve the killing of an innocent person. It had been accepted by the court that the twins were two persons in law. The doctors were under a duty to Mary not to carry out the operation because it would kill Mary, but they were under a duty to Jodie to operate because not to operate would kill her.

In this seemingly irreconcilable conflict, the doctors, like the court, had to balance the welfare of each child against the other child and make a decision based on the lesser of two evils. Carrying out the operation could be justified as the lesser of two evils and would not be unlawful. The operation would not offend the sanctity of life principle because Mary was, in effect, slowly killing Jodie and doctors could come to Jodie's defence by carrying out the operation. A majority of the court said that the defence of necessity could be used to justify the murder of Mary. The decision is based on a Utilitarian approach rather than a duty to respect human life. The operation to separate the twins was later carried out and, as a result, Mary died.

The Court of Appeal decided against treatment in the following case and followed the wishes of the parents in refusing medical treatment. In *Re T (A Minor) (Wardship: Medical Treatment)* (1997), T was born with a liver defect and, without a transplant, would only live for two years. Doctors said that the operation would be successful and believed that it was in the baby's best interests. The parents, who both worked in the health service, refused to consent to the transplant and moved abroad. The local authority applied to the court under the Children Act 1989 for the court to exercise its inherent jurisdiction. The High Court held that the mother had acted unreasonably and overruled the parents' refusal of treatment. The Court of Appeal said that the most important consideration was the welfare of the child. It was important not to base the decision simply on the medical assessment of the situation, namely, that the operation would succeed. The mother knew that the baby only had a short time to live without a transplant and wanted the baby to continue his peaceful and painless life. The fact that the mother had refused treatment for the baby also had to be considered, as the mother would have to look after the baby after an operation. Further, the disruption to the whole family in moving back to England for the operation had to be taken into account. The court concluded that it was in the best interests of the baby to leave his treatment in the hands of his parents.

Parents requesting treatment against medical advice

Sometimes, parents disagree with medical staff and want their child to have treatment. In *Re C (A Minor) (Medical Treatment)* (1998), C suffered from a deteriorating condition and the doctors considered that any treatment would simply be delaying death. They wished to withdraw ventilation and, if C suffered further breathing difficulties, they did not wish to ventilate her. The parents agreed to withdrawing ventilation but wanted it to be given again if needed, because, as Orthodox Jews, they believed that life had to be preserved. The High Court had to consider what was in the best interests of the child. It took account of the medical evidence that further treatment would be futile and granted an order that ventilation could be withdrawn.

This case illustrates that the courts will not order treatment against the wishes of medical staff. More recently, in *R v Portsmouth Hospital NHS Trust* (1999), a child born with cerebral palsy was now 12 years old. After a tonsillectomy, he suffered from various infections; doctors considered that the child was dying and wanted to stop treatment and give him diamorphine to alleviate his pain. This was against the wishes of the parents. The parents then intervened to stop the administration of diamorphine and to resuscitate the child. Following this incident, the hospital wrote to the parents, saying that the child should be treated elsewhere if further treatment was needed. His mother applied for judicial review of the lawfulness of the hospital's actions in withdrawing lifesaving treatment against the wishes of the parents. The application was dismissed at first instance and the mother appealed to the Court of Appeal for leave to appeal. The Court of Appeal said that, if the parents did not agree with medical staff, then, in serious cases, the matter had to go to court and the court could decide what was in the best interests of the child. Using judicial review should be a last resort, as more suitable remedies were available. These included a specific issue order under s 8 of the Children Act 1989 or a declaration about a proposed course of action; alternatively, the child could be made a ward of court. It would not be helpful to set out guidance, as the considerations with such children were infinite.

Limits on parents' powers to consent to treatment

The right of parents to consent to treatment for their child must be exercised in the 'best interests' of the child. Clearly, consenting to routine medical treatment which will benefit the child is within the parents' powers. But can parents consent to other treatment, such as major surgery, sterilisation, cosmetic surgery, circumcision, medical research or transplants?

The result of a sterilisation operation is that a woman cannot have children. The right to bear children is seen as a fundamental human right. In *Re D (A Minor) (Wardship: Sterilisation)* (1976), D was an 11 year old girl who suffered from 'Sotos syndrome', which meant that she developed physically at a young age. She also suffered from epilepsy, was mentally deficient and had behavioural problems. The child's mother was worried that D might become pregnant and that D would not be able to look after a child. D would not be able to manage contraception and the mother wished to have her sterilised. A doctor agreed to carry out the operation but an educational psychologist disagreed and applied to the court to make D a ward of court. The High Court said that a sterilisation operation was irrevocable. D could not understand the implications of having such an operation. However, in the future, it was likely that D would have a greater understanding of such an operation and would then be able to make her own choice. The operation was not medically necessary and sterilisation for non-therapeutic purposes was not in D's best interests.

This can be contrasted with *Re B (A Minor) (Wardship: Sterilisation)* (1988), which concerned a 17 year old patient, B, who lived in a residential home. She had a mental age of five or six and suffered from epilepsy, rendering her virtually unable to communicate. Although she was sexually mature, she had no understanding of the link between sex and pregnancy and her mother was worried that B might become pregnant, as she would not be able to manage contraceptives. If she became pregnant and needed a Caesarean operation, this would lead to problems, as she had a habit of picking at wounds. The mother and the local authority applied to the court for an order that the sterilisation would be lawful. The House of Lords said that B would never understand what was involved and would never be able to make a choice herself.

This case can be distinguished from *Re D* (1976). Here, B could not be seen as having a right to bear children, as she had no understanding of the concept. If B became pregnant, this would seriously affect her health. Sterilisation was allowed. Lord Templeman said that, in his opinion, a girl under 18 should not be sterilised without the permission of the court.

A distinction can be made between sterilisation which is needed as part of therapeutic medical treatment and sterilisation for social purposes. In the latter case, the opinion of the court should be obtained. In *Re E (A Minor) (Medical Treatment)* (1991), a 17 year old mentally handicapped girl had menstrual problems, which could only be solved by a hysterectomy. The court said that:

> ... there is a clear distinction to be made between cases where an operation is required for genuine therapeutic reasons and those where the operation is designed to achieve sterilisation.

The consent of the court was not needed and the parents could consent.

A Practice Note on sterilisation was issued in 1996 (*Official Solicitor: Sterilisation* [1996] 2 FLR 111). Applications for minors should go to the Family Division of the High Court under its inherent jurisdiction, or under the Children Act 1989 for a specific issue order under s 8. The preferred course is under the inherent jurisdiction.

Can parents consent to cosmetic surgery for children? If the child has an obvious facial blemish or 'bat ears', then the parents can consent. A balance has to be struck between the child undergoing the treatment and the pain and suffering such treatment entails, and being left without the treatment, thus having to suffer unwanted attention and 'offensive' remarks.

Female circumcision is a criminal offence, unless the operation is necessary for therapeutic purposes, as provided by s 1 of the Prohibition of Female Circumcision Act 1985.

Male circumcision is practised in some cultures. In *Re J (A Minor) (Specific Issue Orders: Muslim Upbringing and Circumcision)* (1999), the father of a Muslim boy wanted to have the boy circumcised but his mother refused. The Court of Appeal said that this was an irreversible procedure and no one with parental responsibility could authorise it against the wishes of another. A court order was needed.

Can parents consent to young children being involved in medical research? If the research is for therapeutic purposes, the parents can consent. Clearly, this will be for the benefit of the child. If the research is for non-therapeutic purposes, then the question is whether any particular procedure is in the child's best interests. This may be difficult to establish if there is no direct benefit to the child. An adult may consent to research on themselves for non-therapeutic reasons, as this may be seen as altruistic. The legal position is not clear as to whether an adult may consent for a child in the same circumstances.

Can parents consent to transplants to or from their child? Such a transplant may involve tissue or organs. A transplant *to* the child will depend on whether it is in the best interests of the child (see *Re T* (1997), where consent to a liver transplant was refused). Transplants *from* children are not covered by the Family Law Reform Act 1969 and the decision would have to be made under common law rules. But could a child be regarded as *Gillick* competent in respect of organ donation? This seems doubtful. Bone marrow transplants by children are not uncommon and parents can give permission for this.

Refusal of treatment by both children and parents

If both the child and the parents refuse treatment, can the doctor carry on with treatment? The doctor would have to explain the consequences of refusing the treatment. The most difficult situation is if the refusal would lead to the death of the patient. In *Re E (A Minor) (Wardship: Medical Treatment)* (1993), a boy aged 15 and three-quarters with leukaemia needed treatment involving blood transfusions. Both he and his parents were Jehovah's Witnesses and they all refused to consent to the treatment. The treatment had an 80–90% chance of success. The boy was made a ward of court by the hospital and, when he was dying, the hospital applied for permission to treat him. The court accepted that the boy was intelligent and had made the decision of his own free will but said that it could override the boy's and his parent's decision. The court said that the boy did not fully understand the implications of dying and, although he had a strong belief, that could change in the future. The court allowed the hospital to treat the boy.

More usually, a court faced by this type of dilemma will find that the child is not competent. In *Re S (A Minor) (Medical Treatment)* (1994), S, a girl aged 15 and a half, had a condition which required daily injections and monthly blood transfusions. When S was 10 years old, her mother became a Jehovah's Witness and took S to meetings. S refused to consent to any further transfusions and the local authority applied to the High Court to use its inherent jurisdiction to override S's refusal. The court said that S was not *Gillick* competent and the doctors were authorised to give transfusions.

Guidance on withholding life prolonging treatment

In 1999, the British Medical Association issued guidance on withholding treatment: *Withholding and Withdrawing Life Prolonging Medical Treatment*. This includes guidance on decisions made in the case of children and young people (see, for example, paras 14–19).

The Human Rights Act 1998

Article 2 (the right to life) could be invoked by a child who needs treatment to save their life, for example, in *Re C (A Child) (HIV Testing)* (1999). In *Re A (Children)* (2000), the court said that the death of Mary as a result of the operation would not be a breach of Art 2. Article 3 (freedom from inhuman and degrading treatment) could be used if treatment is given against the wishes of the child. The court did not consider that the proposed operation could be regarded as inhuman and degrading to Mary under Art 3.

Article 9 (freedom of religion) could be used in cases where a child is given treatment against his religious beliefs, as in the case of Jehovah's Witnesses who are given blood transfusions. However, a conflict may arise in such cases between the right to life and freedom of religion. It would then be up to the court to decide which should prevail. A conflict may also arise between the views of the parents, as in *Re J* (1999), where the father was in favour of circumcision but the mother was against it. The court said that, if there was a conflict between two parents or between the parents and the child, the court could impose limitations and act in the best interests of the child.

4 Medical Negligence

You should be familiar with the following areas:

- the extent of the duty of care in negligence
- factors relevant in deciding whether there was a breach of duty
- requirements for causation: 'but for' test; remoteness
- requirements for claims in nervous shock
- *res ipsa loquitur*; contributory negligence; limitation; vicarious liability

Introduction

In 1980, the combined medical defence unions, which defend doctors in negligence claims, reported that the payment of damages in negligence claims had reached a total of £1 million in that year. Recently, the Medical Defence Union reported that the amount paid out in damages for 1999 was £77 million, compared to £41 million in 1996 ((2000) 144(31) SJ 743). It has recently been estimated that the NHS owes approximately £3 billion in compensation to victims of medical negligence. There are many reasons for the growth in negligence claims, the main ones being the greater awareness that people have of their rights to claim, the desire to blame someone if something should go wrong and the belief that doctors and hospitals should be able to 'cure' patients. The development of medical technology has meant that riskier and more invasive procedures can be carried out. As life expectancy increases, the diseases and problems of old age create more claims. New services, for example, NHS telephone advice lines, also create the potential for claims arising from negligent advice or misdiagnosis. Some lawyers specialise in medical claims and lawyers giving advice in such cases now have to be on a specialist panel approved by the Law Society. Cases may also be brought on a conditional fee basis, which means that the claimant does not have to worry about paying legal bills if they lose their case.

Nonetheless, there are still particular difficulties with bringing successful claims as a result of negligent medical treatment, and claimants who bring their claim on this basis are less likely to win than general negligence claimants. When things go wrong, many patients (or their relatives) simply want an explanation, rather than taking legal action, and, in providing explanations, hospitals can reduce the number of claims made.

Medical negligence is not regarded as a particular type of civil wrong in its own right – it is simply the general rules of the tort of negligence applied to medical accidents. If someone suffers an injury in the course of treatment under the NHS, they can bring a claim in negligence. They cannot claim for breach of contract because a patient does not have a contract with the NHS (see above, Chapter 1).

Elements of the tort of negligence

The claimant who wishes to bring a claim in negligence has to meet the requirements set out by the House of Lords in *Donoghue v Stevenson* (1932). The claimant's friend bought her a bottle of ginger beer in a café. As the claimant was drinking the ginger beer, she saw the remains of a snail in her glass, was promptly sick and suffered shock. The House of Lords said that a manufacturer owed a duty of care to the ultimate consumer, because the manufacturer should reasonably have foreseen that, if he was careless in making the ginger beer, someone drinking it would suffer harm. Lord Atkin set out the 'neighbour principle':

> You must take reasonable care to avoid acts and omissions which you can reasonably foresee would be likely to injure your neighbour.

The court set out the three requirements for a successful claim in negligence:

(a) the defendant owed the claimant a duty of care;

(b) the defendant broke that duty of care; and

(c) the defendant's breach of duty caused the damage to the claimant.

The duty in negligence applies to both acts and omissions.

(a) The duty of care

There is no general duty on doctors to provide treatment for people; for example, a doctor who is watching a film at the cinema does not have to help someone who faints. The claimant must establish that the defendant doctor owes the claimant a duty of care. The 'universal test' for establishing a duty was set out in *Marc Rich v Bishop Rock Marine* (1995) and the three factors of foreseeability, proximity and just and reasonableness have to be proved. Proving that a duty is owed does not usually cause any problem, as the duty of a doctor (or other health staff) to a patient is well established.

It may be more of a problem to pinpoint when that duty arises. Is this when the patient:

- telephones for an ambulance?;
- arrives at the hospital in an ambulance?;
- arrives at the hospital entrance?;
- reports to reception?;
- is given treatment?

A duty would certainly be owed to a patient arriving in an ambulance or reporting to reception. A patient who simply walks into the hospital may have difficulty showing that a duty is owed to them at that point. The courts have been reluctant to make the emergency services liable in negligence for policy reasons, as illustrated by *Capital Counties v Hampshire CC* (1997), where the court said that the fire service could only be liable if they made an error which no reasonable fire service would make and which made the position worse. In *Kent v Griffiths and The London Ambulance Service* (2000), the pregnant claimant suffered an asthma attack and called her doctor, who arrived at the house, examined the claimant and dialled 999 for an ambulance. The ambulance took nearly 40 minutes to arrive and, because of the delay, the claimant suffered respiratory arrest and a miscarriage. The claimant sued the doctor and the ambulance service for negligence and the ambulance service argued that it was not legally bound to respond to an emergency call and could only be liable if it made the claimant's position worse by a negligent act. The Court of Appeal said that the ambulance service was part of the NHS and should be seen as providing services similar to hospitals, rather than the police or the fire brigade. Once an emergency call was accepted, a duty of care was owed and the defendant was liable. It was accepted that there was no question of an ambulance not being available in this case.

The normal doctor-patient relationship gives rise to a duty of care in tort, but what of a relationship outside this context? If an employer asks a doctor to carry out a medical examination of a job applicant and the doctor does this negligently, the doctor owes a duty of care to the employer. If, as a result, the applicant does not obtain the job, they can sue the doctor for economic loss. What is the position if the doctor simply gives advice based on the applicant's medical record? In *Kapfunde v Abbey National plc* (1998), the defendants sent the claimant's completed application form to a doctor, who acted as their independent advisor. The claimant had stated that she had been off work with sickle cell anaemia and the doctor advised the defendants that she was unsuitable. The defendants refused to employ the claimant and she sued the doctor in negligence. The Court of Appeal said that, even if it was foreseeable that the claimant would suffer financial loss if the doctor was careless, there was no direct doctor-patient relationship and the doctor had not assumed a duty to the claimant. The doctor was not liable.

In *N v Agrawal* (1999), the defendant doctor examined the claimant, who was a suspected rape victim, but did not appear at the trial as a witness. The claimant argued that the doctor owed her a duty of care to attend and, because of breach of this duty, the trial collapsed and the claimant suffered psychiatric harm. The Court of Appeal held that, in carrying out such an examination, the doctor did not assume responsibility for the claimant's psychiatric welfare and the doctor-patient relationship did not arise. The duty was simply to take care during the examination in not making the claimant's position worse. There was not sufficient proximity to create a duty of care. The court used the analogy of a doctor who witnesses a road accident and gives assistance – there, no doctor-patient relationship arises.

(b) Breach of the duty of care

The second matter for the claimant to prove is that the doctor is in breach of his duty of care. The question which needs to be addressed is, what standard of conduct does the doctor have to reach to fulfil the duty? The usual standard used in the tort of negligence is the standard of the 'reasonable man', which is an objective standard. But this does not work if the defendant has a particular skill, because the reasonable man does not have that skill. Instead, the law applies the '*Bolam* test'.

In *Bolam v Frien HMC* (1957), the claimant was mentally ill and was given electro-convulsive therapy. At the time, patients having this treatment were given relaxant drugs or were physically restrained, or neither of these. The claimant was given treatment without drugs or restraints and, as a result, broke his hip. The court said that a doctor was not negligent if he acted in accordance with 'a responsible body of medical men' and, as he had done this, he was not liable.

A doctor does not have to reach the standard of the 'best' doctor, but simply the average, competent doctor in that particular field. A GP will be judged by the standard of a competent GP and is not expected to reach the standard of a specialist surgeon.

Factors relevant in determining the standard of care

National Health Service Acts
These set out various statutory duties. For example, under s 1 of the National Health Service Act 1977, the Secretary of State for Health is under a duty to provide 'a comprehensive health service'. Attempts have been made to enforce these statutory duties, but without success (see, for example, *R v Central Birmingham HA ex p Collier* (1988)). The question here is whether a failure to fulfil a statutory duty can also lead to breach of a duty in negligence. In *Re HIV Haemophiliac Litigation* (1990), haemophiliacs were given contaminated Factor VIII, which gave them the AIDS virus. They argued that there was a breach of statutory duty and negligence. The court said that there was not a breach of statutory duty, but that in itself did not preclude a claim in negligence. A successful claim in negligence is not, therefore, ruled out, but it seems remote.

Professional codes
These are guidelines produced by various medical professional bodies, such as the General Medical Council. Breach of a code is not negligence in itself but will be relevant in deciding whether someone has acted in breach of duty.

Keeping up to date
All medical staff must keep up with major developments in their particular specialism. For example, a cancer specialist must know about important new treatments. The courts accept, however, that medical staff cannot be expected to know about every new

development. In *Crawford v Charing Cross Hospital* (1953), the claimant developed paralysis because his arm had been put at a right angle to his body during an operation. An article in *The Lancet* six months previously had pointed out this danger. The court held that it would be impossible to require doctors to read every article in the medical press. The anaesthetist had not read the article but was not negligent.

At the present time, the vast amount of medical literature and research and the advent of the internet make it impossible for any individual to keep up with all current developments in their field, but they do need to know about major changes. Mason and McCall-Smith warn that 'It is no longer possible for a doctor to coast along on the basis of long experience' (*Law and Medical Ethics*, 5th edn, 1999, Butterworths).

Following a general practice

It will usually be a good defence that medical staff have followed the generally accepted practice. The first matter to establish is that there was an accepted practice. In *Roe v Minister of Health* (1954), Roe went into hospital in 1947 for an operation and was given a spinal anaesthetic (nupercaine). The anaesthetic, in ampoule form, was kept in a clear solution of phenol but tiny cracks in the ampoules had let phenol in, which contaminated the anaesthetic. As a result of being given the anaesthetic, Roe was paralysed from the waist down. It was held by the Court of Appeal that the defendants had followed the normal practice and no one could have foreseen the risk, so they were not negligent. Denning L.J. said: 'We must not look at the 1947 accident with 1954 spectacles.' Clearly, after this accident, hospitals had to change the practice and Denning LJ pointed out that, after the accident in 1951, a leading medical textbook had warned that keeping the anaesthetic solution in a clear spirit so that cracks could not be seen could cause permanent paralysis. He added, 'Nowadays it would be negligence not to realise the danger, but it was not then'.

Different medical opinions

In medical matters, it is common for there to be different opinions. If a doctor follows a minority practice, is this negligent? In *Maynard v West Midlands RHA* (1985), doctors believed that the patient had tuberculosis, but symptoms showed that it might be Hodgkin's disease, which is fatal unless treated quickly. Instead of waiting for the test results for tuberculosis, the doctors carried out an exploratory operation to see whether the patient had Hodgkin's disease, which in fact showed that he had tuberculosis. The operation caused damage to a nerve, even though it was carried out without negligence. However, the patient claimed that the operation was not necessary and that it had been negligent to carry it out. The House of Lords said that this was not negligent, as a competent body of medical opinion would have agreed with this course of action. Lord Scarman quoted the words of Lord President Clyde in *Hunter v Hanley* (1955):

> In the realm of diagnosis and treatment, there is ample scope for genuine differences of opinion and one man clearly is not negligent merely because his conclusion differs from that of other professional men. The true test for establishing negligence in diagnosis or treatment on the part of a doctor is whether he has been proved to be guilty of such failure as no doctor of ordinary skill would be guilty of if acting with ordinary care ...

In *Bolitho v City and Hackney HA* (1992), Dillon LJ in the Court of Appeal said that a court could reject a body of medical opinion if the court considered that it was '*Wednesbury* unreasonable', that is, that it was a view which no reasonable body of doctors would have held.

New treatments
The law has to allow medical staff to try new procedures and new drugs, otherwise developments would be stifled. In deciding whether a new treatment was negligent, the courts have to take account of whether existing treatments had failed; what would happen to the patient without trying the new treatment; and the risks to the patient of having the new treatment. In *Clark v MacLennan* (1983), the claimant suffered incontinence after the birth of a child and normal treatment failed to work. A gynaecologist then carried out a procedure which left the claimant with permanent incontinence. This procedure would not normally have been tried until three months after the birth. It was held that the doctor should have waited, and it was negligence to depart form the normal practice.

Misdiagnosis
A mistake in diagnosing a medical condition is not in itself negligent. Many conditions have similar symptoms – see, for example, *Maynard v West Midlands RHA* (1985), above. A doctor is judged by the '*Bolam* test' of what a competent doctor would do in the circumstances. This will involve looking at medical notes, asking the patient questions, carrying out an examination of the patient and, if necessary, carrying out tests or X-rays. In *Wood v Thurston* (1951), the claimant was taken

to hospital by his friends. He was in a drunken state and his friends told the doctor that the claimant had been seen under a moving lorry. He was examined, his facial cuts were dressed and he was sent home in a taxi. A few hours later, he died, and it was found that he had broken most of his ribs and his collarbone and had a congested lung. The doctor argued that he was not liable because the claimant's drunken state had dulled his reaction to pain. It was held that this was negligence, as the claimant's condition could easily have been detected by using a stethoscope. In *Langley v Campbell* (1975), a GP who failed to diagnose malaria in a patient who had recently been to Africa was held to be negligent.

Particular knowledge of the claimant

If medical staff have particular knowledge about a patient, this may mean that a higher duty of care is owed to that patient – for example, if a patient is very young, very old, has particular allergies, is known to be violent, etc. In *Selfe v Ilford and District HMC* (1970), a 17 year old boy was admitted to hospital after taking an overdose. He was put in a ward on the ground floor with 27 patients and three nurses. One nurse went to the toilet, one went to make tea and one was called to a patient. The boy then climbed out of an open window and onto the roof, and jumped off. As a result, he was paralysed. It was held that the hospital was negligent, as it knew that he was a suicide risk and not enough supervision had been provided. However, the courts have accepted that supervision cannot be provided at every moment. In one case, a patient suffering from mental deficiency went to the toilet, ate a lavatory freshener and died. This was held not to be negligence.

Particular characteristics of the patient

If a patient has particular characteristics which make treatment more difficult, these are taken into account. In *Williams v North Liverpool HMC* (1959), the defendants gave the claimant an injection into the arm tissue instead of a vein and this caused an abscess. It was held that, because the patient was overweight and it was difficult to find a vein, the defendants were not liable.

Failure of communication between staff

The practice of medicine has always involved teamwork, and this, in turn, relies on communication of information between medical staff. Particular problems arise if patients are transferred to other hospitals. In *Coles v Reading HMC* (1963), the claimant's finger was crushed in an accident at work. He went to a small local hospital, where his wound was cleaned and dressed, and was told to go to Reading Hospital for further treatment. Instead, he went home and, some time later, the wound became infected and he died of blood poisoning. It was held that the local hospital had been negligent, as the claimant should have been given a note by the local hospital referring him to Reading Hospital for further treatment and should have been told to go there immediately. This was a failure by the doctors to communicate with each other.

Newly qualified staff

It is not a defence to a claim for negligence that the doctor has recently qualified. The law applies an objective standard and, under the *Bolam* test, a doctor must reach the standard of a competent and experienced doctor. In *Wilshire v Essex AHA* (1987), Mustill LJ said that the standard of care is defined by the particular post that the doctor occupies, rather than the status of the doctor in the hospital hierarchy. A doctor in a specialist baby unit would need to reach the standard of an experienced doctor in such a unit. Although this seems harsh, the standard may be reached through supervision or by a young, inexperienced doctor asking a consultant for advice.

Alternative medical practitioners

What standard should be applied to someone practising a different type of medicine from the normal, orthodox type? Is it enough to judge them by the standard of the competent practitioner of that type of medicine? In *Shakoor (Deceased) v Situ* (2000), the deceased consulted the defendant about a skin condition which needed surgery using orthodox medicine. The defendant, who practised Chinese herbal medicine, prescribed a herbal remedy. After taking nine doses, the deceased suffered liver failure and died. His widow sued for negligence. The evidence showed that the remedy had produced a rare reaction which could not be predicted. The claimant argued that the defendant was negligent in prescribing the remedy or for not warning of the risk of liver damage. The court said that the defendant owed a duty of care to the deceased and the question was, what criteria should be used to decide whether the defendant was in breach of his duty: the standard of the careful practitioner of Chinese herbal medicine or the standard of orthodox doctors? A practitioner of herbal medicine practised alongside orthodox medicine and this had to be taken into account. This was an internal remedy and the practitioner had to have regard to the following:

- he worked in a system of law and medicine, which would review the standard of care;

- the practitioner had a duty to ensure that any remedy was not harmful;

- he must realise that someone suffering an adverse reaction would go to an orthodox hospital and such incidents might appear in medical journals.

It was up to the practitioner to check that there were no adverse reports, or to subscribe to a body that checked for him. The defendant had acted in accordance with the standard of care required to practise Chinese herbal medicine and was not liable.

Lack of resources

If a hospital is sued for negligence, could it claim that it was a lack of resources which led to a lower standard of care, and that, therefore, they should not be liable? It is a feature of the NHS that funds are short and there is frequently a shortage of staff, beds or equipment (or all three!). It would not be acceptable for a hospital to rely on lack of resources as a defence to a claim for negligence, because, if a particular service was provided, the hospital would have to reach the *Bolam* standard for that service. If they could not reach the *Bolam* standard, then they should not provide that particular service. For example, if a hospital could not provide an accident and emergency service to the *Bolam* standard, they should not provide one. The situation can be illustrated by *Bull v Devon AHA* (1993), where the claimant was pregnant with twins. A problem arose with the delivery of the second twin and there was a delay of over one hour in the attendance of a suitably qualified doctor because facilities were on two sites and, under the system operated by the defendants, doctors were not available quickly enough. As a result of the delay, the second twin was born with brain damage. The court said that a proper system needed to be in place if maternity services were provided. In practice, a hospital facing a shortage of resources or staff would withdraw certain facilities, for example, by closing a particular ward. It would have been better in the circumstances if the hospital had not provided facilities for childbirth.

Duty to third parties

In tort, as a general rule, a person is not liable for an injury caused to another by a third party. In *Smith v Littlewoods* (1987), a third party set fire to the defendant's disused cinema and the fire damaged the claimant's property next door. It was held by the House of Lords that the defendants were not liable, as, even though the damage was foreseeable, the defendants did not know about the third party and an intolerable burden would be imposed on owners of property if a duty was found in these circumstances. There are exceptions to this rule where:

- there is a special relationship between the claimant and the defendant;

- there is a special relationship between the defendant and third party; or

- the defendant creates the danger.

In *Palmer v Tees HA* (1999), an inpatient at the defendant's mental hospital threatened to kill a child in June 1993. Shortly after this, he was released and became an outpatient. Over a year later, the patient abducted and murdered the claimant's daughter and, as a result, the claimant suffered nervous shock. The patient lived in the same street as the child he murdered. The Court of Appeal considered whether proximity could be established between the claimant and the defendant. The claimant victim had to be identified and, clearly, the defendant could not do this. What precautions could the defendant have taken? It was difficult to detain outpatients. The best precaution was to warn the victim, but the defendant did not know who to warn. In the circumstances, the defendants could not be liable.

Another possibility is that a doctor or hospital gives advice to a patient, which the patient acts on and which causes harm to a third party. Does a doctor owe a duty to the third party? In *Goodwill v BPAS* (1996), the defendant carried out a vasectomy for M. Three years later, M, a married man, started a relationship with the claimant. He told her about his vasectomy. The claimant became pregnant and sued the defendants for the cost of bringing up the child. The Court of Appeal applied the principles from *Hedley Byrne v Heller* (1964), saying that, in a claim for financial loss, the claimant had to show that the defendant knew that the advice was likely to be acted on and had been acted on. It was held that the defendant could not reasonably foresee that the claimant would act on their advice, as they did not know about M's future sexual partners and there was no assumption of responsibility to the claimant. The claimant could obtain independent advice herself. The defendants were not liable.

(c) Breach caused damage

The claimant must prove that the defendant's breach caused the damage. Two matters must be proved:

(a) as a matter of fact, the defendant's breach caused the claimant's loss; and

(b) the damage was not too remote.

Point (a) is known as causation in fact. The courts use the 'but for' test to determine whether the defendant caused the loss, that is, would the claimant have suffered loss but for the defendant's negligence? If the answer is 'no', then the defendant must logically have caused the harm and is liable. The operation of this test can be seen in *Barnett v Chelsea Hospital* (1969). Three night watchmen called at the hospital's casualty department early one morning, complaining that they had been vomiting since drinking tea at 5 am. The nurse contacted the duty doctor, who advised that they should go home and see their own doctor. A few hours later, one of the men died. It was discovered that they had mistakenly put arsenic in their tea but, even if they had been admitted to the hospital, the deceased would have died, because it would have taken some time to diagnose the problem. The widow sued for negligence. It was held that the defendants owed a duty of care to the deceased and they had broken that duty by sending him away without an examination. If the test was applied – would the deceased have died 'but for' the negligence of the defendants? – the answer would be 'yes'. Therefore, the breach did not cause the death because he would have died anyway. The hospital was not liable.

There are often problems in proving causation in fact in medical cases because there may be a number of causes for illnesses and medical conditions. There is the added requirement that it is up to the claimant to prove his case on the balance of probabilities, which is often difficult in medical matters. In *Kay v Ayrshire and Arran Health Board* (1987), the claimant was a two year old boy who was admitted to hospital with suspected meningitis and was given an overdose of penicillin. The boy later became deaf and claimed that the overdose caused the deafness. It was held that the evidence showed that it was probably the meningitis, not the overdose, which caused the deafness.

A similar result occurred in *Wilsher v Essex AHA* (1988), where the claimant was born prematurely. A junior doctor mistakenly put a catheter into a vein instead of an artery and the baby was given too much oxygen. The baby later went blind. One of the possible causes was too much oxygen and the claimant sued. The House of Lords said that, although too much oxygen caused blindness, there were four other possible causes and the baby had these four conditions. It was not possible for the claimant to show that the blindness was caused by too much oxygen.

In *Bolitho v City and Hackney HA* (1997), the claimant, a boy aged two who had breathing difficulties, was taken to the defendant's hospital. He suffered acute shortage of breath and the nurse summoned the doctor, but the doctor did not attend. Later, the boy had a similar shortage of breath and suffered cardiac arrest and brain damage. The claimant argued that failure to attend was negligent. The defendant accepted this but said that it was not liable because, even if the doctor had attended, she would not have intubated him and he would still have suffered brain damage. Each side called experts to show that a responsible body of medical opinion would intubate and would not intubate. The House of Lords held that the defendant was not liable in negligence, as a responsible body of medical opinion would not have intubated the boy. Lord Browne-Wilkinson said:

> ... the judge, before accepting a body of opinion as being responsible, reasonable or respectable, will need to be satisfied that, in forming their views, the experts have directed their minds to the question of comparative risks and benefits and have reached a defensible conclusion on the matter.

Effectively, what the House of Lords are saying is that the courts have the ultimate decision as to whether an act is negligent or not. *Bolitho* was applied in *Marriott v West Midlands HA* (1999), where the claimant fell downstairs at home in 1984 and injured his head and was unconscious for 20–30 minutes. He was taken to hospital and X-rays of his skull were taken, but no abnormalities were noticed and he was discharged. A week later, his condition had not improved and he still had headaches, and so his GP (the third defendant) was called. The GP examined the claimant but tests showed no abnormality. A few days after this, the claimant's condition deteriorated and he was admitted to hospital. He was found to have a fractured skull and had sustained a haematoma; he was left disabled. The claimant argued that the GP was negligent in failing to realise the claimant's position and in failing to send him back to hospital. Experts were called for each side to give evidence of what a GP should do in such circumstances. The judge agreed with the claimant's expert – a doctor seeing such a patient who had shown no improvement and was suffering from headaches ought to send the patient to hospital. The defendant's body of professional opinion was not reasonably prudent. On appeal, the Court of Appeal said that the judge could subject medical opinion to analysis to see if it was reasonable, and was entitled to find that it was unreasonable. The appeal was dismissed.

The Court of Appeal reiterated that expert medical evidence of sound medical practice had to be capable of withstanding logical analysis in *Penney, Palmer and Cannon v East Kent HA* (2000), which involved the negligent reading of cervical smears by the defendants, resulting in the claimants being wrongly told that they were free of cancer.

If the damage was caused by more than one factor, the 'but for' test does not work. Instead, the law asks the question, did the defendant's act 'materially contribute' to the claimant's damage? If the answer is 'yes', the defendant is liable (*Mc Ghee v NCB* (1972)). In *Wilsher v Essex AHA* (1988), the claimant was unable to prove that giving the baby too much oxygen made a 'material contribution' to the blindness. A difficult case in this area is *Hotson v East Berkshire AHA* (1987), decided by the House of Lords. The claimant, a 13 year old boy, fell out of a tree and was taken to hospital, but he was sent home. Five days later, he returned to hospital and an X-ray showed that he had a fractured hip. He developed avascular necrosis, a deformity of the hip joint. The defendants admitted negligence in not diagnosing the injury but argued that the condition was not caused by the delay. It was held by the High Court that, if the claimant's condition had been diagnosed immediately, there was still a 75% chance that the condition would occur. The defendant's breach had caused the loss of a 25% chance of recovery and the claimant was entitled to 25% compensation. The House of Lords said that the claimant had to prove that the delay in treatment was a material cause of the condition. The evidence was that the fall damaged blood vessels and this caused the condition. The claimant was not entitled to any compensation, as he was not able to prove on a balance of probabilities that, but for the delay, his injury would have healed without developing the condition. He could not prove this on a balance of probabilities because, statistically, he only had a 25% chance of recovery. The claimant was trying to claim for the loss of the chance of recovering. But the claimant's argument was based on a hypothetical situation because, even if he had been treated immediately, he may have been in the group (the 75%) which would not have made a full recovery. However, the House of Lords did not say that a claim for loss of a chance could never succeed.

In *Chappell v Hart* (1999), H had a pharyngeal pouch, a condition which would eventually need surgery. The operation had a risk of damage to the oesophagus, leading to infection and damage to the voice. C did not warn H of this risk and, although C carried out the operation carefully, H's voice was damaged. H claimed that if she had been warned, she would have waited and had the operation performed by the best specialist. H was awarded damages. C appealed, arguing that there was no causal connection between the failure to warn and the injury, because, as surgery was inevitable, H had lost nothing because she had not lost the chance of the risk being avoided. Also, the injury resulted from a random risk which H accepted. The High Court of Australia dismissed C's appeal. They said that the claim was for physical injury, not the loss of a chance. The injury was foreseeable, C had a duty to warn H of the risk and the injury would not have happened without C's breach of duty; therefore, C's breach caused the damage. The fact that H would have been exposed to the risk later did not mean that she would have suffered it, and *Hotson v East Berkshire HA* (1987) could be distinguished.

Even if the claimant establishes factual causation it still has to be proved that the defendant's act is a legal cause of the harm (point (b) in the two stage causation test). This is also known as the principle of remoteness. The defendant cannot be made liable for everything which happens as a result of a negligent act. The law uses this principle to limit liability. Applying the rule from *The Wagon Mound (No 1)* (1961), the test for determining whether the damage is too remote is the test of reasonable foreseeability. The courts often use this requirement to deny liability on policy grounds.

The thin skull rule

The thin skull rule can be explained by the principle, 'you must take your victim as you find him'. The effect of this is that, if the claimant has a special sensitivity and suffers more serious harm than a normal person, the defendant is liable for all of that harm. Even though the extra harm is not foreseeable, the defendant is liable. The rule protects sensitive claimants. The classic example is *Smith v Leech Brain* (1961), where, due to the defendant's negligence, the husband of the claimant suffered a small burn on his lip. This caused a latent cancer to develop and the husband died. The defendants were held liable. Similarly, in *Robinson v Post Office* (1974), due to the defendant's negligence, the claimant slipped at work and cut his leg. He was given an anti-tetanus injection by a doctor but he was allergic to this and suffered brain damage. The court said that the defendants had to take the claimant as they found him and they were liable for the full extent of the injuries.

Examples of where the thin skull rule applies would include patients with allergies, weak hearts, brittle bones and haemophilia.

Res ipsa loquitur

The normal rule is that it is up to the claimant to prove, on a balance of probabilities, that the defendant has been negligent. Sometimes, the claimant will be able to rely on the principle of '*res ipsa loquitur*' (the thing speaks for itself). The circumstances when this will apply are when it is obvious that the defendant has been negligent. The requirements to establish it are:

(a) there is no explanation for the injury; and

(b) such an injury would not normally happen if care is taken; and

(c) the defendant had control of the 'instrument' causing the damage.

This principle does not reverse the burden of proof and it is still up to the claimant to produce evidence to show that the defendant is liable. In *Cassidy v Ministry of Health* (1951), Lord Denning said that the claimant could say, 'I went into hospital to be cured of two stiff fingers. I have come out with four stiff fingers and my hand is useless. That should not happen if due care had been used. Explain it if you can'.

The principle has not been used often in medical cases, but the typical example is *Mahon v Osborne* (1939). The claimant had an abdominal operation and, two months later, it was found that a swab had been left in his body. As a result of this, he died. It was held by the Court of Appeal that *res ipsa loquitur* applied and the surgeon was liable.

In *Leckie v Brent and Harrow AHA* (1982), the claimant suffered a 1.5 cm cut to her cheek while her mother was having a Caesarean section. It was held that *res ipsa loquitur* applied and, in the absence of an explanation, the surgeon was negligent.

Contributory negligence

Under s 1(1) of the Law Reform (Contributory Negligence) Act 1945, if the defendant can show that the claimant has been partly to blame for the injury, then the compensation payable may be reduced to the extent the court believes it is just and equitable. Under s 1(2), the court should assess the total damages and then make the reduction.

Contributory negligence could arise in medical cases, for example, if a patient discharged themselves from hospital against medical advice and suffered harm as a result. The courts have been reluctant to say that a claimant has been contributorily negligent. In *Coles v Reading HMC* (1963), even though the claimant had failed to go to the main hospital for further treatment when told to do so by his doctor, he was not considered to be contributorily negligent. Medical staff must be on the alert for patients who are reluctant to follow advice or co-operate with treatment. As patients now have more say about their treatment, it is possible that the courts may find them contributorily negligent in appropriate circumstances.

The Limitation Acts

The law limits the time period within which a claimant must bring his claim because of difficulties of proof many years after the event and because it is unfair that someone should have a potential claim outstanding for an indefinite period. The effect of the limitation period is that it provides a defence for a defendant against whom a claim is made. Under s 11 of the Limitation Act 1980, if the claim is for personal injuries, the claim must be brought (a) within three years from when the cause of action accrued; or (b) three years from the date of the claimant's knowledge of the right of action, whichever is later. Under s 14, the date of knowledge is when the claimant had, or should have had, knowledge that the injury was significant and that it was attributable, wholly or in part, to the act, and knowledge of the identity of the defendant. The test used by the courts is what a reasonable man would have known, but this is given a subjective element, as the claimant's age, intelligence, etc, is taken into account. In *Spargo v North Essex DHA* (1997), the claimant was detained in a mental hospital for 22 years after being diagnosed as suffering brain damage as a result of dieting. Five years after leaving hospital, the claimant saw a solicitor, claiming that she had been misdiagnosed. She did not issue a writ (now a claim form) until 12 years after leaving hospital. The Court of Appeal held that she realised the connection between the hospital's negligence and her suffering when she saw her solicitor. She had three years from that time and, therefore, had left it too late.

Under s 33 of the Limitation Act 1980, the court has a discretion to extend the three year period if there are valid reasons for the delay and if it would be just in all the circumstances. In *Das v Ganju* (1999), the claimant's daughter was born severely disabled in 1978 because the claimant had had German measles during the pregnancy. In 1988, her lawyers wrongly told her that her claim was not for personal injury and that it was too late to sue. The claimant consulted new solicitors and, in 1996, 18 years after the birth, the claimant sued the defendant doctor for failing to warn her that a rash in pregnancy could have been German measles. The defendant argued that the claim was too late. The Court of Appeal, in exercising its discretion under s 33, took into account the fact that the claimant had been given the wrong legal advice and that she was not at fault. It allowed the claim to proceed.

For other tort claims, the limitation period is fixed at six years from when the right of action accrued under s 2 of the Limitation Act 1980. One example would be a claim for economic loss (financial loss) for the cost of bringing up a child after a failed sterilisation. This fixed period also covers intentional torts, for example, assault. In *Stubbings v Webb* (1993), W was abused by her stepfather in 1971 but did not realise that this abuse caused her psychiatric problems until 1984, when she consulted a psychiatrist. In 1987, when she was 30 years old, she issued a writ. The House of Lords held that s 11 did not apply to intentional acts and s 2 gave a fixed period of six years, which could not be extended. W had to sue within six years of reaching 18 and was therefore outside the limitation period. This is clearly a disadvantage for someone suing under the six year period, as no extension may be given.

If someone is under a legal disability, for example, if they are under 18 years old or of unsound mind, the limitation period runs from when the disability ends or when they die, whichever occurs first. For example, in the case of a minor suing for personal injuries caused by medical negligence when they were 10, the limitation period is three years after their 18th birthday (as in *Stubbings v Webb*).

If the claimant dies before the three year limitation period expires, a new period of three years runs from the date of death or the date of the personal representative's knowledge of the right to sue, whichever is later.

It should be noted that the Limitation Act 1980 also fixes a six year period for claims in contract.

Vicarious liability

One problem faced by a patient bringing a claim in negligence will often be whom to sue. A patient who is treated in a hospital may have been injured by a doctor, nurse, radiologist, physiotherapist, etc. Under the principle of 'vicarious liability', an employer is liable for the torts of employees which are committed 'in the course of employment'. An employer is not liable for the negligent acts of an independent contractor. Rather than suing the individual member of staff for negligence, the patient can sue the hospital using the principle of vicarious liability. To establish vicarious liability, it must be shown that *the tort was committed by an employee*. The law developed a number of tests to determine whether someone is an employee, including the control test, the organisation test and the multiple test. Most of the staff in a hospital will clearly be employees and will be full time, but what is the position of a consultant surgeon who works at the hospital for one day each week? In *Roe v Minister of Health* (1954), Denning LJ said:

> I think that the hospital authorities are responsible for the whole of their staff ... It does not matter whether they are permanent or temporary, resident or visiting, whole time or part time. The hospital authorities are responsible for all of them. The reason is because, even if they are not servants, they are the agents of the hospital to give the treatment.

The legal position of agency staff who are taken on by the hospital on an *ad hoc* basis is unclear – for example, nurses hired from an agency. They may be seen as employees because of the control exercised over them by the hospital. Alternatively, the nurse may be seen as an agent of the hospital, which would then be liable for her torts.

The tort must be *committed in the course of employment*. If a nurse carried out an operation on a patient and the patient was harmed, then this would not be in the course of the nurse's employment. The hospital may, however, be made liable for negligence in allowing such a situation to arise.

In applying the above principles to a hospital situation, the patient can sue the hospital (or the health authority) and does not need to identify the individual responsible for the negligent act. In fact, the individual member of staff is also liable in tort and it would be possible to sue that individual, although it would be unusual to do so, as they would be unlikely to be able to pay compensation.

It has been argued that a hospital owes a non-delegable, direct duty to patients. In *Ellis v Wallsend District Hospital* (1989), the Australian courts held that a direct duty was owed by the hospital where a patient went directly to the hospital for treatment. This principle of direct liability may also apply in English law, although the point has not been directly addressed. In *Wilsher v Essex AHA* (1987), in the Court of Appeal, Lord Browne-Wilkinson said: 'I can see no reason why, in principle, the health authority should not be [directly] liable if its organisation is at fault.' It can be argued, therefore, that a health authority is directly liable for providing medical care to patients and will be liable for breach of that duty. The principle of direct liability is more likely to apply if there is negligence in the organisation and management of the hospital, rather than in the actual provision of treatment.

If the patient was injured by a GP (family doctor), then that individual doctor is liable, rather than the health authority, as the GP is an independent contractor. The GP is vicariously liable for the actions of the staff of the practice. Hospital doctors are covered by the NHS indemnity scheme, but GPs are not covered by the scheme and have to insure against claims through their professional bodies.

Negligent misstatements

Most negligence claims involve the commission of a negligent act, but negligence may also take the form of negligent advice. Negligent advice may lead to physical injury or, more usually, economic (that is, financial) loss. In *Hedley Byrne v Heller* (1963), the House of Lords said that, if a 'special relationship' could be established between the claimant and the defendant, in that the defendant knew that the claimant would rely on the advice, and the defendant assumed responsibility, the defendant could be liable. A doctor giving advice to a patient would have a special relationship with that patient and would owe them a duty not to give negligent advice. It is likely that negligent advice would lead to physical injury, for example, if a doctor told a patient to put butter on a burn and this caused further harm. A doctor may also be liable to a third party in respect of that advice if the requirements of *Hedley Byrne v Heller* are met. Such a claim was made in *Goodwill v BPAS* (1996) (see below).

Nervous shock (psychiatric injury)

Nervous shock, or psychiatric harm, means some medically recognised psychiatric illness which results from being exposed to an accident caused by the defendant's negligence. It does not include normal grief or shock, for which no claim can be made. Following the Hillsborough football tragedy, many relatives of the victims suffered nervous shock, although they lost their claims in the courts (*Alcock v Chief Constable of South Yorkshire Police* (1991)). In *Page v Smith* (1995), the House of Lords set out two categories of claimants:

(a) primary victims, who are at the scene of the event and within the range of foreseeable physical harm. The claimant must show that the defendant could foresee 'personal injury'.

(b) secondary victims are those who are not directly involved but suffer shock as a result of what they see or hear.

In *Alcock v Chief Constable of South Yorkshire Police* (1991), the Hillsborough case, the Court of Appeal set out the requirements for a secondary victim to claim:

- there had to be a relationship of 'love and affection' between the claimant and the victim;

- the claimant had to be present at the accident or in the aftermath – in *Alcock*, relatives who suffered nervous shock after identifying bodies eight hours afterwards were not considered to be present in the aftermath;

- the claimant must see or hear the event or aftermath – being told by someone else is not sufficient;

- there must be a sudden shock – so seeing something on television would not be sufficient.

With secondary victims, the claimant must show that the defendant could foresee nervous shock. In addition, the claimant has to show that a person of 'reasonable fortitude' would have suffered nervous shock.

In a medical context, it is unlikely that someone would have a claim as a primary victim unless they were present at the time of the negligent act and within range of harm. Someone may claim as a secondary victim – for example, if a child dies as a result of negligent medical treatment and the parents suffer nervous shock, they may have a claim. In *Sion v Hampstead HA* (1994), the claimant's son died as a result of negligent medical treatment and the claimant suffered nervous shock after visiting his son in hospital over a period of two weeks before the son's eventual death. The Court of Appeal said that there was no sudden shock and the claim failed.

In the *Creutzfeldt-Jakob Disease Litigation Group B, Plaintiffs v Medical Research Council and Secretary of State for Health* (2000), the claimants suffered from dwarfism. By 1 July 1977, the defendants knew that a drug, HGH, which was used to treat dwarfism, carried a risk of CJD. However, the defendants used HGH in clinical trials on the claimants after 1 July. The claimants later discovered, either from their doctors or from the media, that CJD could be fatal. They suffered nervous shock as a result of knowing that they might develop CJD. It was held that the defendants could have realised that injections of HGH could have led to CJD and it was reasonably foreseeable that patients would be given this news over a wide time span. The risk of the claimants suffering psychiatric injury as a result of learning about CJD was reasonably foreseeable. Claimants who could prove nervous shock caused by knowledge of the risk of CJD were entitled to compensation.

The Law Commission has issued a Report on *Liability for Psychiatric Illness* (No 249, 1998), in which it is argued that the law is too restrictive and claims for nervous shock should be made simply on the basis of the requirement of love and affection. Under the proposed legislation (the Negligence (Psychiatric Illness) Bill), there is no need to show that the psychiatric illness was induced by shock. The Law Commission proposes that liability should be based on 'a close tie of love and affection' between the claimant and the victim and that there is no need for the claimant to prove that they were close to the accident or the aftermath in both time and space, as required by *Alcock v Chief Constable of South Yorkshire Police* (1991).

The Law Commission has set out a list of relationships where a close tie of love and affection is presumed. These are spouse, parent, child, brother or sister and a cohabitant of at least two years' standing. Claimants outside this list would have to establish a close tie of love and affection, for example, grandparents.

The Consumer Protection Act 1987

Patients may be given a wide variety of medical products in the course of their treatment. These can include drugs, blood, artificial limbs, heart pacemakers, etc. In June 2000, patients who were given breast implants filled with soya oil were warned that there was a risk they could cause cancer, and they were advised to have them removed. Patients who suffer harm as a result of being provided with a product may have possible claims in contract, in negligence and under the Consumer Protection Act (CPA) 1987. If the product is supplied under the NHS, then no claim can be made in contract. If the product is supplied in the course of private treatment, a claim in contract could be made. However, an NHS patient could bring a claim for negligence at common law and would have to prove duty, breach and damage (*Donoghue v Stevenson* (1932)). Another possibility is to bring a claim under the CPA 1987 for harm caused by a 'defective' product.

The CPA 1987 was passed to implement the European Community Product Liability Directive (85/374/EEC). There are some differences in wording between the Directive and the CPA, but s 1 of the latter provides that the Act must be interpreted so as to comply with the Directive.

The CPA makes the producer strictly liable for harm caused by defective products. Under s 2(1), 'where any damage is caused wholly or partly by a defect in a product, every person to whom subsection (2) applies shall be liable for the damage'. A person claiming under the CPA must prove that: (a) the product was defective; (b) damage was suffered; and (c) the damage was caused by the defect. This last requirement still poses a problem for claimants in, for example, proving that a drug caused particular side effects.

Product

Under s 1(2) of the CPA 1987, 'product' is defined widely, to include any goods, components and raw materials incorporated in other products. 'Goods' is further defined as including any substance or growing crops. However, it is undecided whether blood or organs are covered by this definition.

Defect

Goods are defective if their safety is not such as persons generally are entitled to expect (s 3(1)). This imposes an objective standard, but the Directive provides that goods are defective if they do not reach the standard that 'a person is entitled to expect', which is a subjective standard and wider than that of the CPA 1987. In deciding whether goods are defective, the courts must take into account all the circumstances, including matters set out in s 3(2), which includes:

(a) the way in which goods are sold and the purposes for which they are sold, for example, for adults or children;

(b) any instructions or warnings – with medicines, it is important to give clear instructions on use and information about side effects because, if this is not done and harm results, the medicine will be treated as a 'defective' product. If the medicines are for children, they may need to be in a childproof container, so that only adults may give the medicine;

(c) what might reasonably be expected to be done with the goods, etc.

A claim was brought under the CPA 1987 in *Richardson v LRC Products Ltd* (2000). After the birth of their second child, the claimant and her husband used condoms, as they did not want any more children. During sex, a condom fractured and the claimant became pregnant. She brought a claim under the CPA 1987, arguing that the condom was a defective product. The court held that, under s 3, in deciding what persons were 'entitled to expect', any instructions and warnings had to be taken into account. The defendants had not claimed that the condoms were 100% effective and evidence showed the inexplicable failure of some condoms. The fracture in the condom did not prove that it was defective. In any event, the claimant could have avoided the pregnancy by taking the 'morning after pill' and her claim failed.

Section 3 adds that the fact that a safer product is produced does not mean that the earlier version was defective. This last requirement was necessary to allow manufacturers to produce improved products, as, without this exclusion, a person with an earlier version could claim that it was defective.

Damage

This covers death, injury or damage to property. However, it does not cover damage to the actual product or any product supplied with the defective product in it (s 5(2)) or damage not exceeding £275.

Producer

The CPA 1987 renders the 'producer' liable, and this covers the manufacturer, the producer of raw materials, the processor, the own brander, the importer into the European Union and the supplier. The supplier is only liable if they do not tell the claimant the identity of the producer, own brander or importer. A hospital or health authority could be liable either as a manufacturer, for example, if it produces its own medicines or artificial limbs, or simply as a supplier. It is important that hospitals keep records which enable their suppliers to be identified, so that, in the event of a claim, liability may be passed on. These records should be kept for 10 years, as liability lasts for 10 years from when the product is put into circulation.

Defences

The CPA also provides a number of defences. The most important one is s 4(1)(e) – the defence that the state of scientific and technical knowledge at the relevant time was not such that a producer of products of the same description might be expected to have discovered the defect. Although this imposes an objective test – that of the 'reasonable producer' – it will be interpreted to comply with the Directive, which refers to knowledge that would enable the producer to discover the defect. This defence effectively allows manufacturers to avoid liability if, at the time that the product was produced, the defect could not have been discovered in the light of the scientific knowledge at that time.

The CPA 1987 amends the Limitation Act 1980 and provides that a claimant must sue within three years of when the damage occurred or the date on which the claimant knew that he had a right of action. This limitation period is subject to a 'longstop' of 10 years from when the product was put into circulation. This 10 year period causes problems with drugs, as their adverse effects may not be realised until many years later.

In medical matters, the main importance of the CPA is with regard to the supply of drugs. Primarily, the manufacturer will be liable for defective drugs, but it is important for hospitals to maintain accurate records and to know who their suppliers are; otherwise, they may be found liable as a 'producer'.

Criminal liability for negligence

If a patient dies as a result of negligent treatment, medical staff could face prosecution for a criminal offence. In criminal offences, the prosecution have to prove two elements: (a) the *actus reus* (guilty act); and (b) the *mens rea* (intention, recklessness or negligence). Possible offences that staff could face are murder or manslaughter.

Murder

Murder is a common law offence and is the unlawful killing of a human being under the Queen's Peace with malice aforethought. The defendant's act must cause the death of the victim. The intention of a doctor is important in deciding whether the act is murder. The *mens rea* is the intention to kill or cause grievous bodily harm. If a doctor gives painkilling drugs which he knows will shorten the victim's life, is the doctor guilty of murder? In *R v Adams* (1957), the court said that, if the purpose was to relieve pain, that was not murder. It is unlikely that a doctor's actions would amount to murder unless the doctor deliberately intended to kill or could foresee that death was highly likely.

Manslaughter

This is a lesser crime than murder and can be divided into two categories:

(a) voluntary manslaughter – the defendant has the *mens rea* for murder but has one of the defences of provocation, diminished responsibility or suicide pact. It would be extremely unlikely for these defences to be relevant to medical staff;

(b) involuntary manslaughter – there are two types: constructive manslaughter and gross negligence manslaughter. Constructive manslaughter is where the defendant commits an unlawful act which causes death. Gross negligence manslaughter is where the defendant acts in breach of duty, and it is this type which is relevant to medical care. In *R v Adomako* (1995), the defendant anaesthetist did not notice that, during an operation the oxygen supply had become disconnected, as a result of which the patient died. The House of Lords said that the defendant had to owe a duty of care to the victim; the death must be caused by breach of that duty; and the breach had to be so bad that it could be described as 'gross'. Here, the oxygen was disconnected for nine minutes and would have been noticed by any reasonably skilled doctor. The defendant was guilty of gross negligence manslaughter.

Mason and McCall-Smith have expressed concern that the criminal courts should be used for maintaining standards in operating theatres.

The Human Rights Act 1998

Article 2 (the right to life) may be used if a health authority fails to make provision for medical care and this failure leads to death, or serious injury which could cause death. Article 3 (degrading treatment) may provide a basis on which to claim in some circumstances. In *D v UK* (1997), a drug smuggler suffering from AIDS was due to be deported to a country with poor medical facilities and successfully claimed that to deport him would be a breach of Art 3. Article 8 (the right to private life) may have implications for mixed wards.

5 Confidentiality and Medical Records

You should be familiar with the following areas:

- common law rules: the duty of confidence; children; incompetent adults
- exceptions to the duty: consent; public interest; public good
- confidentiality and HIV
- is there a duty to disclose?
- statutory exceptions
- remedies: damages; injunctions
- medical records

Introduction

The duty of confidence requires that doctors must keep information about their patients secret. This duty has a long history and is part of the Hippocratic oath:

> All that may come to my knowledge in the exercise of my profession or outside my profession or in daily commerce with men, which ought not to be spread abroad, I will keep secret and will never reveal [Hippocrates, c 420 BC].

The Declaration of Geneva 1948 (amended at Sydney 1968) is a modern, international version of the Hippocratic oath and states, 'I will respect the secrets which are confided in me, even after the patient has died'. The main ethical theories also support the duty of confidence. From a utilitarian viewpoint, patients are more likely to give information to doctors if they know that they have a duty of confidence, and this leads to better overall health for the population at large. From a deontological (or duty-based) point of view, the principle of respect for autonomy requires a doctor to keep information about patients confidential. The effect of the Human Rights Act 1998 means that Art 8 of the European Convention on Human Rights (the right to respect for private life) will require a person's medical records to be kept private. Professional codes produced by medical and nursing bodies require members to keep information about patients obtained in the course of their work confidential. The common law rules also require information obtained in certain circumstances to be kept confidential. The common law rules were not developed specifically with regard to medical information but apply generally.

The duty of confidence is not an absolute duty and even the Hippocratic oath reflects this. The law has had to develop exceptions to the duty, and these will be examined below.

The common law rules

The common law recognises that, in certain circumstances, a duty of confidence may arise. The requirements for bringing a claim for breach of this duty were set out in *AG v Guardian Newspapers (No 2)* (1988). Lord Goff said that there is a duty of confidence if confidential information comes to the knowledge of someone in circumstances where that person has notice that the information is confidential and it would be just not to disclose that information. He went on to say that there was a 'public interest' in maintaining a duty of confidence. If personal medical information is given by a patient to a doctor in the course of the doctor-patient relationship, a duty of confidence arises in favour of the patient.

What is the scope of this duty of confidence?

If medical information is given without disclosing the name of the patient, is this a breach of the duty of confidence? In *R v Department of Health ex p Source Informatics Ltd* (2000), SI Ltd wanted information on the prescribing habits of GPs which it could sell to pharmaceutical companies. SI Ltd made an agreement with pharmacists that, for a fee, the pharmacists would provide SI Ltd with information which was taken from prescription forms. This information included the names of GPs and the types and quantities of drugs prescribed, but not the names of the patients. The pharmacists did not give the names of the patients, as SI Ltd was only interested in knowing about the prescribing habits of GPs. The Department of Health issued a policy document stating that, even though this information was anonymous, it could be a breach of the duty of confidence. SI Ltd applied for judicial review, claiming that this policy was wrong. At first instance, the application was dismissed and the court said that the patient would not have consented to the information being passed to SI Ltd and there was no public interest to override the duty of confidence. In the Court of Appeal, judgment was given by Simon Brown LJ, who set out the requirements for a duty of confidentiality, as established in the judgment of Megarry J in *Coco v AN Clark (Engineers) Ltd* (1969):

(a) the information must have the quality of confidence;

(b) the information must be given in circumstances implying an obligation of confidence;

(c) there must be an unauthorised use of the information.

The court said that the patient had no proprietary right in the prescription form or the information on it and, therefore, had no right to control its use if privacy was not at risk. The patient's privacy was protected here and there was no breach of the duty of confidence by the pharmacists.

If confidential information can be disclosed because it comes within one of the exceptions, this does not mean the information can be disclosed to anyone. The disclosure may only be made to an appropriate person for particular purposes. In *Woolgar v Chief Constable of Sussex Police* (1999), the claimant nurse had been arrested after the death of a patient but was later released without being charged with any offence. The nursing regulatory body, the UKCC, also investigated the matter and asked the police for a copy of the statement made by the nurse. The nurse would not consent to this disclosure and, when the police said that they would pass on a copy of the statement, the nurse sought an injunction. The Court of Appeal held that the police could pass this information to the UKCC because the issue of public safety overrode the duty of confidence.

Medical information given to the doctor by a patient is confidential, but what of other information? In *R v Wilson* (1996), the defendant had branded his wife's bottom with his initials, at her request. He was convicted of actual bodily harm under s 47 of the Offences Against the Person Act 1861. The police obtained the information from a medical report made by the wife's doctor. This would be a breach of the duty of confidence if it was given without consent, because it was information given to the doctor in the course of a medical consultation.

Particular difficulties occur with some categories of patients:

(a) Children: children are owed a duty of confidence, to the extent that their medical records cannot be disclosed to strangers, but what about giving information to their parents? With young children who lack the capacity to consent to treatment, the doctor will need to tell the parents about the treatment which he proposes to give the child, as the doctor must act in the best interests of the child. The parents have a legal duty to look after the child and need to know about the child's health.

But what is the position with older children? A '*Gillick* competent' child can consent to treatment and it may be argued that disclosure of medical information about that child to the parent would be a breach of the duty of confidence. However, if a child refuses treatment, the doctor may ask the parent for consent, and this may mean that medical information about the child is given to the parent. If the child consents to treatment but asks the doctor not to disclose this to his parents, then, strictly, the doctor should not tell the parents. The normal exceptions to the duty of confidence apply and, for example, a child may consent to disclose to their parents.

(b) Incompetent adults: the legal position on disclosing confidential information is unclear. It may be argued that a duty of confidence can be implied from the fact there is a doctor-patient relationship. Some guidance may be gleaned from *Re F* (1990): with incompetent patients, treatment may be given in the best interests of the patient and, by analogy, medical information may only be disclosed if it is in the patient's best interests to do so.

(c) Dead patients: can medical staff disclose confidential information about a patient after the patient's death? The duty of confidence arises from the personal relationship between the doctor and the patient and, therefore, it can be argued that the legal duty of confidence ends on the patient's death. General Medical Council (GMC) guidance, *Confidentiality: Protecting and Providing Information* (2000) states:

> 40 You still have an obligation to keep personal information confidential after a patient dies. The extent to which confidential information may be disclosed after a patient's death will depend on the circumstances. These include the nature of the information, whether the information is already public knowledge or can be anonymised, and the intended use

to which the information will be put. You should also consider whether the disclosure of information may cause distress to, or be of benefit to, the patient's partner or family.

However, Mason and McCall-Smith point out that the death certificate is a public document and it gives the cause of death, which is not then confidential. This can have repercussions for the family if, for example, the patient has died of AIDS (see *Law and Medical Ethics*, 5th edn, 1999, Butterworths, p 213).

Exceptions to the duty of confidence

(a) Consent
The patient may consent to disclosure of their medical information. This consent must be given freely. Mason and McCall-Smith (*Law and Medical Ethics*, p 194) say that such consent is not always given freely:

> What patient at a teaching hospital outpatient department is likely to refuse when the consultant asks: 'You don't mind these young doctors being present, do you?' – the pressures are virtually irresistible and truly autonomous consent is impossible, yet the confidential doctor-patient relationship ... has, effectively, been broken.

The consent to disclosure may be expressly given or may be implied. A patient may expressly consent to relatives being told about their condition. Obviously, any patient going to a hospital for treatment may need a number of medical staff to look at their notes. For example, if the patient has a suspected broken leg, the notes will be passed to a radiologist. Consent to this may be implied. But what limits are there as to who, within the hospital, should see the information? Professional associations recognise that information must be given to other members of a medical team. The GMC's guidelines allow other healthcare professionals to be given information:

Sharing information with others providing care
7   Where patients have consented to treatment, express consent is not usually needed before relevant personal information is shared to enable the treatment to be provided. For example, express consent would not be needed before general practitioners disclose relevant personal information so that a medical secretary can type a referral letter. Similarly, where a patient has agreed to be referred for an X-ray, physicians may make relevant information available to radiologists. Doctors cannot treat patients safely nor provide

continuity of care, without having relevant information about the patient's condition and medical history.

8 You should make sure that patients are aware that personal information about them will be shared within the health care team, unless they object, and of the reasons for this. It is particularly important to check that patients understand what will be disclosed if it is necessary to share personal information with anyone employed by another organisation or agency providing health or social care, except where this would put others at risk of death or serious harm.

9 You must make sure that anyone to whom you disclose personal information understands that it is given to them in confidence, which they must respect. Anyone receiving personal information in order to provide health care is bound by a legal duty of confidence, whether or not that they have contractual or professional obligations to protect confidentiality.

(b) Public interest

Sometimes, it is in the public interest to breach the duty of confidence. An example of this would be where a patient had committed a serious crime which was disclosed in the course of medical treatment. The leading case is *W v Egdell* (1990). W was convicted of killing five of his neighbours and was detained in a secure hospital under the Mental Health Act 1983. Some time later, he applied to a mental health review tribunal to be moved to another hospital. His lawyer obtained a report from Dr E, but this stated that W had an obsessive interest in firearms and explosives and was dangerous. W wished to obtain an injunction to prevent the use of the report. W withdrew his appeal to the tribunal but Dr E sent a copy of his report to both the head of the secure hospital and the Home Office. The Court of Appeal said that Dr E *did* owe a duty of confidence to W. But here, there were two conflicting public interests. One was that mental patients should be free to seek medical advice and to make full disclosure to doctors. They would only be able to do this if there was a duty of confidence owed to them and they were certain that information divulged would be kept secret. Secondly, there was the public interest in the fact that W was a dangerous patient and, if released, would be a risk to the safety of the public. The court has the task of balancing these interests and, in this case, decided that the disclosure by Dr E was justified. Bingham LJ said:

There is one consideration which, in my judgment, as in that of the judge, weighs the balance of public interest decisively in favour of disclosure. It may be shortly put. Where a man has committed multiple killings under the disability of serious mental illness, decisions which may lead directly or indirectly to his release from hospital should not be made unless a responsible authority is properly able to make an informed judgment that the risk of repetition is so small as to be acceptable.

Sir Stephen Brown in the same case said that the risk must be 'real, immediate and serious'. It is unclear whether all three of these requirements would have to be met; if so, it limits the circumstances in which disclosure can be made.

The courts also take notice of guidelines from the professional medical bodies in making decisions. The GMC's *Confidentiality: Protecting and Providing Information* (2000) states:

Disclosures to protect the patient or others

36 Disclosure of personal information without consent may be justified where failure to do so may expose the patient or others to risk of death or serious harm. Where third parties are exposed to a risk so serious that it outweighs the patient's privacy interest, you should seek consent to disclosure where practicable. If it is not practicable, you should disclose information promptly to an appropriate person or authority. You should generally inform the patient before disclosing the information.

The UKCC's *Guidelines For Professional Practice* (1996) state:

The public interest means the interests of an individual, or groups of individuals or of society as a whole, and would, for example, cover matters such as serious crime, child abuse, drug trafficking or other activities which place others at serious risk.

Shortly after *W v Egdell*, in *R v Crozier* (1990), the defendant had been charged with attempted murder and employed a psychiatrist to prepare a report to be used in his case. The report was not used and the defendant was given a prison sentence. The psychiatrist then gave the report to the prosecution and the judge. The defendant was detained under a hospital order. The defendant appealed, claiming that this breach of the duty of confidence meant that he did not have the choice in deciding whether or not to use the report. The Court of Appeal said that there was a public interest in the disclosure of the report and the psychiatrist had acted reasonably.

There are a number of other questions arising from similar circumstances which remain unresolved. What would the position be as regards the duty of confidence if a patient in the community came to the doctor and it was discovered the patient was dangerous? Is disclosure justified to detect or prevent crime?

What would the position be if the detained person in W's position had committed lesser offences? It would seem that disclosure would not then be justified.

What is the position if a patient has committed a civil wrong? Would this justify breaching a duty of confidence? It seems unlikely that, in normal circumstances, this would override the public interest in a duty of confidence.

(c) Public good

Confidential medical information may be disclosed in circumstances where doing so is for the public good. In *Lion Laboratories v Evans* (1985), confidential documents in the possession of the manufacturers of an intoximeter showed that it was not accurate. The intoximeter readings were used to bring prosecutions for drinking and driving. It was held by the Court of Appeal that there was an important public interest in the disclosure of that information. This case shows that it is not necessary that an offence has been committed or is likely to be committed if there is a legitimate public interest which needs protection.

Confidentiality and HIV

The spread of the HIV infection has caused particular problems with regard to the duty of confidence. The fact that there is no known cure and that AIDS sufferers are likely to be ostracised puts the disease in a category of its own. The main dilemma it poses is, should the duty of confidence be strictly maintained for AIDS patients, or should the duty be broken? If confidence is maintained, then others may unwittingly be exposed to the disease, but, if others are told about a patient with AIDS, would this result in fewer AIDS sufferers asking for medical help? Although AIDS is not a 'notifiable disease', the Minister of Health has the power under regulations to make sufferers have treatment and, if necessary, be detained. The policy behind this approach is that making AIDS a notifiable disease would make people reluctant to go for treatment. The result of this approach is that the duty of confidence is maintained for AIDS patients.

This dilemma was addressed in *X v Y* (1988). An employee of a health authority wrongly disclosed to a newspaper the names of two GPs who were HIV positive but who continued to practice. The health authority sought an injunction to prevent the newspaper from publishing the names. The court had to balance the competing public interests. On the one hand there, is public interest in knowing which doctors are HIV positive and the freedom of the press. On the other is the public interest that those with HIV should be able to obtain confidential medical help. The court held that the risks to patients from HIV doctors were very small and that the interest in publication was outweighed by the special need for confidentiality with HIV positive patients. Rose J said:

> The public in general and patients in particular are entitled to expect hospital records to be confidential and it is not for any individual to take it upon himself or herself to breach that confidence whether induced by a journalist or otherwise.

GMC guidance provides, 'Only in the most exceptional circumstances, where the release of the doctor's name is essential for the protection of patients, may a doctor's HIV status be disclosed without his or her consent' (*HIV Infection and AIDS: The Ethical Considerations* (revised 1993)). Mason and McCall-Smith point out that this policy is 'unworkable', because health authorities are under a duty to tell patient contacts of the infected doctor.

The Department of Health has issued guidelines on dealing with health staff with AIDS: *AIDS/HIV Infected Health Care Workers: Guidance on the Management of Infected Health Care Workers and Patient Notification* (1999). Provision is made for an occupational health physician to co-ordinate matters:

> 10.2 Every effort should be made to avoid disclosure of the infected worker's identity, or information which would allow deductive disclosure.

Particular problems with the duty of confidence occur where a patient is HIV positive. Can the doctor tell the patient's sexual partner? The GMC's *Serious Communicable Diseases* (1998) gives the following guidance:

Giving information to close contacts

> 22 You may disclose information about a patient, whether living or dead, in order to protect a person from risk of death or serious harm. For example, you may disclose information to a known

sexual contact of a patient with HIV where you have reason to think that the patient has not informed that person, and cannot be persuaded to do so. In such circumstances you should tell the patient before you make the disclosure, and you must be prepared to justify a decision to disclose information.

The advice to medical staff when dealing with a patient who has the HIV virus is to try to persuade them to tell their sexual partner. If they refuse, then, under the above guidance, the doctor can tell the partner if he knows the specific individual at risk. However, legally, the matter has not been decided and it could be seen as a breach of the duty of confidence. The court would have to consider the balance between the the two private interests: the patient's right to confidence and the sexual partner's right not to be exposed to the risk of a fatal disease. The court would probably be in favour of disclosure but the issue has not been decided.

Can the doctor tell other health staff?

The GMC guidance when dealing with a patient with HIV or other communicable disease is to tell the patient the full implications of having HIV, how to protect others from the disease and the importance of other health staff knowing about the disease in order to provide proper care.

Serious Communicable Diseases states the following:

19 If patients still refuse to allow other health care workers to be informed, you must respect the patients' wishes except where you judge that failure to disclose the information would put a health care worker or other patient at serious risk of death or serious harm.

In order to provide the most appropriate treatment, it is important that the patient's GP knows that the patient has HIV, but, if the patient does not want them to be told, that confidence must be respected by the hospital unless the GP is exposed to a serious risk by not knowing.

Is there a duty to disclose confidential information to a third party?

If a doctor knows that the patient has HIV or that the patient has threatened to kill someone, is the doctor under a duty to warn that third party? This point has been decided in the US in *Tarasoff v Regents of the University of California* (1976). In August 1969, P told his psychologist, Dr M, that he intended to kill T, another student, who had rejected his sexual advances. Dr M asked the campus police to detain P, which they did for a short time and then released him. In October 1969, P killed T and her parents claimed negligence for failing to warn and failing to detain. The court said that, as a general rule, there was no duty to control another's conduct or to warn third parties about such conduct. But there are exceptions if the defendant has a 'special relationship' with the person who needs to be controlled or the foreseeable victim.

The public interest in effective treatment of mental illness and confidentiality had to be balanced against the public interest in protection from violence. Here, the balance was in favour of protection from violence. There was a special relationship between Dr M and P and the doctor knew that P was a serious danger to T. The doctor was under a duty to take reasonable care to protect the victim. This could be by a warning to the victim, or to friends of the victim or to the police. Here, Dr M was in breach of that duty and the defendants, his employers, were liable.

A more recent example is *Garamella v New York Medical College* (1999). In 1985, Dr DeMasi, a psychiatrist employed by the first defendants, enrolled to study psychoanalysis at the first defendants' college. As part of the course, Dr DeMasi was required to undergo 'training psychoanalysis', which was carried out by Dr Ingram (the second defendant), one of the first defendant's staff. Dr Ingram was under a contractual duty to tell the first defendants if Dr DeMasi was having the required personal psychoanalysis and whether he was ready to be certified as a psychoanalyst. During the psychoanalysis, Dr DeMasi disclosed to Dr Ingram that he was a paedophile. Dr Ingram ended the sessions but did not tell the first defendant either this or the fact that Dr DeMasi was unsuitable to work with children. In 1986, the claimant, a child who attended the hospital for treatment, was sexually assaulted by Dr DeMasi, who was later convicted for this offence. The claimant sued for personal injury. The court said that Dr DeMasi had threatened to harm children and would be working with them. Dr Ingram was responsible for certifying Dr DeMasi's fitness on the training programme and, therefore, had a duty to warn the New York Medical College that the training psychoanalysis was not progressing satisfactorily. The claimant was one of a foreseeable class of victims and Dr Ingram owed the child a duty of care. Although there was a conflict between the public policies of confidentiality and reporting child abuse, a psychiatrist had a duty to disclose when harm to identifiable victims was reasonably foreseeable.

The English courts would be reluctant to impose such a duty. The general rule in negligence is that a person is not liable for the acts of a third party. In *Palmer v Tees HA* (1999), an outpatient who was being treated for mental illness by the defendants had threatened to kill a child. The claimant's four year old daughter was abducted and murdered by the patient and the claimant suffered nervous shock. Three days later, she saw the body of her daughter. The Court of Appeal considered whether a duty could be owed to the claimant. First, the claimant victim had to be identified and here the defendants did not know whom the patient would attack. Secondly, what precautions could the defendant have taken? The powers to detain outpatients are limited and the best thing to do would have been to warn the victim, but the defendants did not know who to warn. Therefore, no duty was owed.

If a doctor discovers in the course of a consultation that a woman patient is being physically abused by her partner, can the doctor inform the police? This would be a clear breach of the duty of confidence. The doctor may only persuade the patient to tell the appropriate authorities. If a doctor discovers that a child patient is suffering abuse, the doctor may tell a third party. The GMC's *Confidentiality: Protecting and Providing Information* (2000) provides:

> 39 If you believe a patient to be a victim of neglect or physical, sexual or emotional abuse and that the patient cannot give or withhold consent to disclosure, you should give information promptly to an appropriate responsible person or statutory agency, where you believe that the disclosure is in the patient's best interests.

Statutory exceptions to the duty of confidence

A number of statutes provide that the duty of confidence may be broken in certain circumstances. The reasons for this vary, from protecting public health to collecting statistics.

Public Health (Control of Disease) Act 1984

Section 10 of this Act lists notifiable diseases, including cholera, plague, relapsing fever, smallpox and typhus. Further diseases have been added by regulations. Under s 11(1):

If a registered medical practitioner becomes aware, or suspects, that a patient whom he is attending within the district of a local authority is suffering from a notifiable disease or from food poisoning, he shall ... send to the proper officer of the local authority for that district a certificate stating –

(a) the name, age and sex of the patient and the address of the premises where the patient is;

(b) the disease or, as the case may be, particulars of the poisoning from which the patient is, or is suspected to be suffering and the date, or approximate date, of its onset ...

The National Health Service (Venereal Diseases) Regulations 1974 provide that any information which would identify an individual who has been examined or treated for any sexually transmitted disease shall not be disclosed. Disclosure may be made to inform a doctor, or someone acting under the direction of a doctor, in the treatment of the patient or prevention of the spread of the disease.

The Abortion Regulations 1991, made under the Abortion Act 1967, require that notice of termination of pregnancy must be given to the Department of Health and to other authorised persons.

There is no general duty on medical staff to assist the police in enquiries by disclosing confidential information, but some statutes create particular obligations.

Prevention of Terrorism Act 1989

Under s 18 of this Act, someone with information which would be of material assistance in preventing an act of terrorism connected with the affairs of Northern Ireland or in securing the conviction of any person for an offence in connection with such an act must disclose the information to a constable as soon as is reasonably practicable.

Road Traffic Act 1988

Section 172(2) of this Act states:

Where the driver of a vehicle is alleged to be guilty of an offence to which this section applies – ...

(b) any other person shall if required as stated above give any information which it is in his power to give and may lead to identification of the driver.

Consequently, a doctor who suspects that a patient has been involved in a traffic accident is under a duty to give information to the police to identify the driver. In *Hunter v Mann* (1974), the court held that this duty was limited to disclosing information which would lead to identification.

Police and Criminal Evidence Act 1984

If the police are investigating a serious offence, they may obtain a warrant to obtain material which would be of use. Under s 9, certain material is 'excluded material' and this would include a patient's medical records, samples of tissue, fluids, etc. In order to gain access to this, the police must apply to a circuit judge.

Remedies for breach of the duty of confidence

The two main legal remedies for breach of the duty of confidence are damages and an injunction to prevent the disclosure of confidential medical information. If a doctor breaches the duty of confidence, the patient may have an action in tort or in contract. A claim in contract may only be brought if there is an existing contract between the doctor and the patient, for example, where the patient is paying for private treatment. This would exclude NHS patients, whose only claim would be in tort. If the claim is in contract, then damages would only be awarded for financial loss, for example, if the patient had lost their job as a result of the breach. As a general rule, a claim for distress or mental harm cannot be made in contract but would have to be made in tort. An injunction could stop disclosure of information, as in *X v Y* (1988), but, if the breach has already happened, an injunction would be too late.

In addition to the legal remedies, a healthcare worker who breached their duty of confidence would face disciplinary action from their professional body, for example, the GMC in the case of doctors.

Access to medical records

Originally, a patient had no right to see their medical records unless disclosure was obtained in the course of a legal claim against the hospital. It was argued against such disclosure that the contents could cause distress to patients, for example, if they had cancer; if records were disclosed, this would stop medical staff from putting in full comments, which would be detrimental to patient health; and, even if disclosure was made, patients would not understand the records. The demand for access to medical records increased in the 1980s and the first step was the Data Protection Act 1984, which gave a right of access to computerised records. This Act has been replaced by the Data Protection Act 1998.

Data Protection Act 1998

This Act was passed to implement European Council Directive 95/46 on the Protection of Individuals in Respect of the Processing of Personal Data. It came into force in March 2000. One important change made by the 1998 Act is that it also governs manually held information, which was not covered by the Data Protection Act 1984. The 1998 Act defines 'data' to include manual data which is part of a 'relevant filing system' from which information is readily accessible. An example of this would be an alphabetical filing system for patients' records. A patient will therefore have access to both computer-held information about them and handwritten medical notes. The Act sets out eight data protection principles, which include the following:

- personal data will be processed fairly and lawfully;

- personal data shall be obtained only for one or more lawful purposes;

- personal data shall be adequate, relevant and not excessive in relation to the purpose for which it is processed;

- personal data shall be accurate and, where necessary, kept up to date.

Section 7 of the Act gives the data subject the right of access to the data, which includes:

- a description of the data;

- the purposes it is being processed for; and

- who it may be given to.

There is also a right to a copy of the data in an intelligible form if a written request is made and a fee paid.

The data subject has the right to change inaccurate data and to claim compensation if damage is suffered as a result of breach of the Act. In addition, breach of the Act is a criminal offence.

Under s 2, 'sensitive personal data' includes information about health and the consent of the data subject is needed to process this data or, if consent cannot be given, processing is necessary to protect the vital interests of the data subject. This exception covers mentally incapacitated adults and children.

The Act applies to existing patient information and not just to data kept after the Act came into force.

Regulations will provide that access can be denied if it would cause serious harm to the physical or mental health of the applicant.

A Data Protection Commissioner is responsible for enforcing the Act.

Access to Medical Reports Act 1988

If someone wants access to a medical report on a person, they must obtain the consent of that person (s 3). This Act gives a patient the right to a copy of a report which is made for employment or insurance purposes before it is sent to the appropriate person. The report will usually be made by the patient's GP. The patient has the right to correct any errors in the report or, if the doctor refuses to change the report, the patient may add their objections to the report. If disclosure of the report would cause serious harm to the physical or mental health of the patient, it can be refused.

Access to Health Records Act 1990

This statute gave patients the right to access medical information kept in manual files. It covers a wide range of health professionals, including doctors, dentists, opticians, chemists, nurses, midwives and physiotherapists. Parents may apply for access to their childrens' medical records but this will only be granted if the child consents or, if the child does not understand the nature of the application, if access is in the best interests of the child.

A child under 16 who is capable of understanding the nature of such an application may obtain access (s 4(1)). The patient is entitled to a copy of the record on payment of a fee. Access may be refused if it would cause serious harm to the physical or mental health of the patient. The patient has the right to change the record if it is not accurate or, if the holder refuses to change it, he may add a comment to the record. The Act does not apply to any records made before 1 November 1991, when the Act came into force. In 1995, a Code of Practice on *Openness* was introduced in the NHS, which allows access to all records made before or after 1 November 1991.

The Human Rights Act 1998

Article 8

1   Everyone has the right to respect for his private and family life, his home and his correspondence.

2   There shall be no interference by a public authority with the exercise of this right except such as is in accordance with the law and is necessary in a democratic society in the interests of national security, public safety or the economic well-being of the country, for the prevention of disorder or crime, for the protection of health or morals, or for the protection of the rights and freedoms of others.

Article 8 is a qualified right and may be restricted in accordance with the provisions of Art 8(2). Medical records are part of someone's private life and disclosure of a patient's records would be a breach of Art 8. In *McGinley v UK* (1999), two ex-servicemen involved in nuclear testing in the Pacific in the 1950s wanted the release of their medical records in order to establish a connection between the testing and cancer. The European Court of Human Rights held that there was no breach of Art 8 on the facts but it said that, in the circumstances of the Government carrying out dangerous activities with serious consequences for peoples' health, those affected had a right to the information. This creates a positive duty of disclosure.

In *R v Secretary of State for the Home Department ex p Belgium, Amnesty International and Others* (1999), the question arose as to whether the Home Secretary could disclose the medical report on Senator Pinochet, which stated that he was medically unfit for trial. Disclosure would be to Belgium, France, Spain and Switzerland but Senator Pinochet refused. The report had been shown to the Chief Medical Officer, who said that the four countries would not be able to prove that it was wrong, and, therefore, there was no reason for disclosing it. The Court of Appeal said that, in such a case, openness was paramount and disclosure was necessary for the prevention of disorder or crime, and they agreed to disclosure. The court considered that disclosure of the medical report was within the exceptions in Art 8(2).

6 Infertility

Introduction

'Infertility' means that a person is unable to have children. This can have a profound effect on both men and women and it is not an uncommon problem – estimates say that one in 10 couples are infertile. Medical advances have brought *in vitro* fertilisation (IVF) treatment and the possibility of using surrogate mothers (substitute mothers). The Warnock Report (*Report of the Committee of Inquiry Into Human Fertilisation and Embryology*, Cmnd 9314, 1984) recommended that reproductive services should be regulated. This was followed by the Human Fertilisation and Embryology Act (HFEA) 1990, which set up a legal framework for infertility treatment and a system of licensing for providers of that treatment. Nevertheless, the law has struggled to keep up with medical developments and the debate on infertility has raised many novel ethical and legal questions. Do people have a right to have children? Do single sex couples have a right to have children? What rights do children born as a result of such treatment have? Who are the legal parents? The Human Rights Act 1998 will also have a significant effect in this area, particularly Arts 12 (the right to marry and have a family) and 8 (the right to respect for private and family life).

The HFEA scheme – outline

Section 5 of the HFEA 1990 provided for the creation of the Human
Fertilisation and Embryology Authority to license clinics for the
purpose of treatment under the 1990 Act and to supervise the services
they provide, to license storage of material and to supervise research.
As regards the provision of infertility services, activities may be
divided into:

- those which are a criminal offence unless carried out under a
  licence, such as creating an embryo outside the body;

- those which are not covered by the Act and are perfectly legal, such
  as artificial insemination by the husband; and

- those which are criminal offences and cannot be licensed, for
  example, cloning.

Section 3 prohibits the creation, keeping or using of an embryo outside
the body without a licence. Section 3(3) prohibits placing an embryo in
an animal, or replacing the nucleus of a cell of an embryo with another
nucleus from a person or embryo (cloning). Section 4 prohibits the
storage and use of any gametes without a licence. In summary, if the
treatment involves creating an embryo outside the body or the use of
stored material, the Act applies. Control over what is done with
donated sperm or eggs is given to the owners, because the 1990 Act
requires the consent of the owner for any use of the gametes. Under
para 1 of Sched 3 to the 1990 Act, a consent must be in writing and, to
be effective, it must not have been withdrawn.

Paragraph 2 provides that consent to the use of any embryo must
specify one or more of the following: use for treatment services to the
person giving consent or that person with another specified person
together; use for treatment to other persons; or use for research. The
consent must also state both the maximum period of storage (the
maximum allowed under the 1990 Act is 10 years (s 14(3)) and what is
to be done with the gametes or embryo if the person giving consent
dies or is incapacitated and cannot alter the consent.

Paragraph 3 provides that, before someone gives consent, they
must be given relevant information and the opportunity for
counselling. Paragraph 4 allows consent to be withdrawn by notice.
Paragraph 5 provides that a person's gametes must not be used for
treatment services unless there is an effective consent and they are
used in accordance with that consent. Paragraph 6 provides that

gametes must not be used for the creation of an embryo unless there is a consent. Paragraph 8 provides that a person's gametes must not be stored unless there is consent for that purpose.

Artificial insemination

If the man is infertile (that is, unable to produce sperm), this problem may be overcome by use of artificial insemination by donor (AID). This method involves semen from the donor being injected into the woman. If the man is impotent (that is, unable to have normal sexual intercourse), his sperm may be injected into his wife artificially (AIH).

(a) By husband (or partner)

This method may or may not involve the help of a doctor. Using this method is not regarded as consummation of the marriage, which may therefore be annulled. If the marriage is annulled, any child born as a result of AIH would be regarded as legitimate, because the parents were married at the time of conception.

One particular problem arises from the practice of 'sperm banking', where sperm may be frozen for future use. This may be used if the husband is going to have a vasectomy or is about to undergo chemotherapy, which could damage his sperm. If the husband dies, the question arises of who then owns the sperm. Section 28(6)(b) of the HFEA 1990 provides that, where sperm is used after a man's death, the man is not to be treated as the father of the child. This stops the child from making any claim against the dead man's estate. However, it is not illegal to use sperm from a dead man.

(b) By donor

This involves the woman being impregnated with sperm from another man, as her partner is infertile. The introduction of a third party raises the question of their legal status in the arrangements. Although the law could not control any private arrangements of this nature, it does control public arrangements, that is, where services are provided to the public. Control of donors is important because of the possibility of passing on genetic defects or disease. A licence is needed under the HFEA 1990 to provide AID services. A man's sperm may only be used if there is an effective consent to that use.

The problems which may arise can be seen in the case of *R v Human Fertilisation and Embryology Authority ex p Blood* (1997). Mr and Mrs Blood wanted to start a family but, before Mrs Blood could become pregnant, Mr Blood caught meningitis and went into a coma. Sperm was taken from Mr Blood and stored and, shortly after this, he died. Mrs Blood then wanted to use the sperm to have a baby but the Human Fertilisation and Embryology Authority refused to allow this because, under s 4(1)(a) of the 1990 Act, there was no licence to store the sperm and, under Sched 3, Mr Blood had not consented in writing to the use of his sperm. Mrs Blood's claim for judicial review failed. She then appealed, claiming that:

- under s 4(1)(b) of the 1990 Act, treatment was allowed without written consent for 'the woman and the man together'; and

- the HFEA's refusal to allow export of the sperm for treatment abroad was a breach of European Union law, which allowed citizens to have medical treatment in any Member State.

The Court of Appeal held that, under s 4(1)(b), treatment could not be regarded as being provided for a woman and man together once the man who had provided the sperm had died. In any case, the exception to written consent only applied if the sperm was used immediately and did not need to be stored, so s 4(1)(b) did not apply. Without a written consent from the husband, the applicant's treatment and storage of the sperm were prohibited under the 1990 Act. However, under the EC Treaty, the applicant had a right to receive medical treatment in another Member State and refusing export of the sperm made fertilisation treatment impossible. The court said that the Human Fertilisation and Embryology Authority had failed to take into account the fact there were unlikely to be any similar cases in the future and the appeal was allowed. The Authority then allowed Mrs Blood to take the sperm abroad.

As regards the legal position of the child born as a result of AID, s 28(2) of the HFEA 1990 provides that, if the parties are married and the embryo was not created with the sperm of the other party to the marriage, that other party shall be treated as the father of the child, unless he did not consent to the insemination. This makes the husband the legal father of the child. Under s 28(3), if the couple are unmarried and treatment services are provided by a licensed clinic 'for her and a man together', and the embryo was not created with sperm from her partner, her partner will be treated as the father of the child. Section 28(4) provides that, where someone is treated as the father of the child under sub-ss (2) or (3), no other person can be treated as the father. This means that the sperm donor cannot be treated as the father if there is already deemed to be a father. Section 28(6) provides that, even if no one is deemed to be the child's father, a sperm donor who gives his consent under the Act is not to be treated as the father. Obviously, if a sperm donor was treated as the father, then there would not be many donors!

The effect of s 28(3) was considered in *U v W (AG Intervening)* (1997). Miss U and Mr W lived together for four years in an 'on-off' relationship. Miss U wanted a child and, because Mr W's sperm was weak, they went to a special clinic in Rome for fertility treatment. They agreed to use donor sperm and signed a form accepting maternity and paternity of the unborn child. Mr W then returned to the UK and Miss U had the treatment. Later, Miss U had twins and claimed that Mr W was the father. The court considered whether s 28(3) of the 1990 Act applied to Mr W. It was argued for Miss U that the requirement for a licence under the 1990 Act was a restriction on the right to medical treatment under Art 59 of the EC Treaty (now Art 49 since the re-numbering of the Treaty, brought about by the Treaty of Amsterdam). It was held that the licensing system did not infringe Art 59 and, although the couple had been treated together, the doctor was not licensed. Therefore, s 28(3) did not apply and Mr W was not the father.

If a single woman requests AID, there are no legal rules to apply and the decision will have to be made on ethical grounds.

Infertile women

A woman may be infertile because of problems in producing ova (eggs) or because of anatomical problems, such as blocked fallopian tubes. The development of IVF means that the ovum may be fertilised in the laboratory and the embryo may then be transferred to the woman's uterus. If the couple are married and the wife's ovum is fertilised with her husband's sperm, the status of the mother, father and child are the same as with a natural birth.

In vitro fertilisation

This process involves taking eggs from the woman, fertilising them with the husband's sperm in the laboratory and then inserting them into the woman's uterus. The first child born in this way was Louise Brown, in 1978. The legal consequences as regards the status of the parties are the same as with AIH, above. The process needs a high level of medical skill and care and it is argued by some that it wastes resources, as the success rate is quite low. The process also requires the transfer of a number of eggs to be successful and sometimes the result is a multiple pregnancy. This in turn may result in the babies dying or the mother being at risk of complications or the mother ending up with several babies to look after.

Ovum donation

If a woman is unable to produce fertile ova, this problem may be overcome by the donation of an ovum by another woman. The donated ovum is fertilised using the husband's (or partner's) sperm and the resultant embryo is then placed in the wife's womb. Under s 27(1) of the 1990 Act, the woman who carries a child as a result of the placing in her of an embryo or sperm and eggs, and no other woman, is to be treated as the mother of the child.

Embryo donation

If both the woman and her husband are infertile, it is possible for donated sperm and ovum to be used to create an embryo *in vitro*. The embryo may then be implanted in the woman. The child born as a result of this procedure is not genetically related to the husband and wife. Legally, the husband will be the father (s 28) and the wife will be the mother under s 27.

Gamete intra fallopian transfer

Gamete intra fallopian transfer (or GIFT) involves taking eggs from an infertile woman and sperm from her husband (or partner). These are mixed together and inserted in the fallopian tubes of the woman to allow fertilisation to take place inside the body. Therefore, under s 1(2) of the 1990 Act, the Act does not apply, as the embryo is not created outside the body. If either the sperm or eggs were donated, then the Act would apply.

Availability of infertility treatment

Should infertility treatment be available for everyone who wants it? If the answer to this question is no, then who should be eligible for treatment? The first restriction is that most types of treatment for infertility are expensive. Additionally, the success rates are not high; for example, only 15% of IVF treatments are successful. Another factor is the age of the woman. The older the woman, the greater the risks in pregnancy and the lower the chances of successfully giving birth to a child. In *R v Sheffield HA ex p Seale* (1994), Seale was a 37 year old woman who wanted IVF treatment but was turned down by the defendant health authority because of their policy of not providing the treatment for women over 35 years of age. It was held that this policy was not unreasonable, given the finite resources of the defendants. Another consideration is provided in s 13(5) of the 1990 Act:

> A woman shall not be provided with treatment services unless account has been taken of the welfare of any child who may be born as a result of the treatment (including the need of that child for a father), and of any other child who may be affected by the birth.

This provision attempts to make the welfare of any child born an important factor in deciding whether someone should be provided with treatment. Kennedy and Grubb point out (*Medical Law, Text with Materials,* 2nd edn, 1994, Butterworths) that, if there is 'an option to bring about the birth of a child, it can never (or almost never) be in its welfare or interests not to be born. Existence for the child is preferable to non-existence'. They argue that the section is about the suitability of the parents. Gillian Douglas informs us that, when the 1990 Act was passing through Parliament, unsuccessful attempts were made to limit treatment to heterosexual couples and s 13(5) was inserted to prevent the creation of single parent families. In a case before the 1990 Act, a claim for judicial review was brought after someone was refused IVF treatment. The applicant was refused treatment after it was discovered that she had a criminal record, including conviction for prostitution. The court held that the criteria applied by the hospital (those used for assessing suitability for adoption) were suitable and that she had had the opportunity to appeal to the hospital against the refusal. Therefore, her claim failed.

The Human Fertilisation and Embryology Authority has produced a *Code of Practice* (4th edn, 1998) which gives guidance on assessing the welfare of the child. Its *Annual Report for 1999* provides as follows:

Clinics must bear in mind such factors as the prospective parents' ages and their likely future ability to look after, or provide for, a child's needs, and any risk of harm to the child or children who may be born. Where the child will have no legal father, clinics must pay particular attention to the prospective mother's ability to meet the child's needs throughout it's childhood.

Many argue that single parents and same sex couples should not be refused treatment. The case of Barrie Drewitt and Tony Barlow in 1999 is examined below.

Anonymity of the donor

There is a deep seated psychological desire for people to know their origins, as evidenced by adopted children trying to trace their natural parents. Should a child have the right to know who their genetic parents are? It is also important for the identity of donors to be kept secret, because, if they were to be made liable for the child which is born, there would be a shortage of donors. How has the law dealt with this conflict? Under s 28(6)(a) of the 1990 Act, where the sperm of a man is used in accordance with the Act, he is not to be treated as the father of the child. The Act makes certain provisions about the anonymity of the donor. Section 31(2) requires the Human Fertilisation and Embryology Authority to keep a register of anyone who provides gametes or who receives treatment services, or anyone who is born as a result of such services. Under s 31(3), if the applicant has reached the age of 18, they may ask the Authority to comply with a request under sub-section (4) and the Authority shall do so if the register shows that the applicant was, or may have been, born as a consequence of treatment services and the applicant has been given notice about counselling.

Under s 31(4), the applicant may ask the Authority to give information about whether the register shows that someone other than a parent of the applicant would or might be a parent of the applicant but for ss 27–29. If the information shows that the applicant might have been born as a result of donated sperm or eggs, the applicant must be told that fact. The applicant cannot be told the name of the donor and the Warnock Committee recommended that this information should not be given. Similarly, the applicant must be told whether someone named, whom they intend to marry, is genetically related to the applicant. Under s 31(5), regulations cannot make the Authority give information about identity prior to those regulations coming into force. At the present time, no regulations have been passed, but, if they are, they cannot apply to those already born. Under s 35, disclosure may be made for the purpose of bringing proceedings under s 1 of the Congenital Disabilities (Civil Liability) Act 1976. A child born disabled as a result of something done in the course of selection, keeping or use outside the body of the embryo or gametes used to form the embryo may sue.

Surrogacy

The word 'surrogate' means 'substitute' and a surrogate mother is someone who has a child for another woman. The basic idea of surrogacy is that one woman (the surrogate) has a baby for a husband and wife (or partners), where the wife is infertile. The surrogate is artificially inseminated with the husband's sperm. When the baby is born, the surrogate mother gives it to the husband and wife (the commissioning parents). In this case, the child is genetically half-related to the husband and wife but there is also a genetic relationship with the surrogate mother, and this is known as a partial surrogacy.

Another possibility is that an embryo is created *in vitro*, using the sperm and egg from the husband and wife, and then the embryo is placed in the surrogate mother. When the child is born, it is given to the husband and wife. Here, the child is genetically related to the husband and wife in the same way as a natural birth. The surrogate mother has no genetic relationship with the child. This is known as a complete surrogacy. There are many other combinations; for example, the commissioning mother may provide the egg or the sperm may be provided by an anonymous donor.

The practice of surrogacy has raised many ethical and legal problems. The Warnock Report (*Report of the Committee of Inquiry Into Human Fertilisation and Embryology*, Cm 9314, 1984) made a number of points about surrogacy: that introducing a third party into the process of procreation was an attack on marriage; the intrusion involved was worse than AID, because the carrying mother made a greater contribution than the sperm donor; a woman should not use her uterus for financial profit (para 8.10). Also, the practice distorts the relationship between the mother and child, because the carrying mother becomes pregnant with the intention of giving away the child; it damages the child, who will have a strong bond with the carrying mother; a surrogacy agreement is degrading for the child, as, effectively, the child is bought for money (para 8.11). The possibility of surrogacy for convenience, where the commissioning mother does not want to go through pregnancy, is ethically unacceptable and is simply treating someone as a means to an end (para 8.17).

The Warnock Report concluded that the main worry was the commercial exploitation of surrogacy, and it recommended:

> ... that legislation be introduced to render criminal the creation or the operation in the United Kingdom of agencies whose purposes include the recruitment of women for surrogate pregnancy or making arrangements for individuals or couples who wish to use the services of a carrying mother [para 8.18].

The Report also said, 'We recommend that it be provided by statute that all surrogacy agreements are illegal contracts and therefore unenforceable in the courts' (para 8.19). However, the Report did not want to make private surrogacy arrangements illegal. It pointed out that, from a deontological (duty) viewpoint, the practice of surrogacy was using the surrogate mother as a means to an end. The Report (para 8.17) also condemned the practice from a utilitarian viewpoint: 'Even in compelling medical circumstances the danger of exploitation of one human being by another appears to the majority of us far to outweigh the potential benefits, in almost every case.'

Arguments for and against surrogacy

For surrogacy:

- helps childless couples;

- encourages altruism, for example, having a child for a friend;

- women should be allowed to do what they want with their own bodies (autonomy);

- gives life to a child.

Against surrogacy:

- it is an unnatural practice;

- it may be seen as selling babies;

- it may be used for convenience, for example, a woman who does not want the 'bother' of pregnancy;

- it splits up the mother and baby;

- women should not sell their bodies for money;
- risks of pregnancy to the surrogate mother;
- harm caused if the surrogate mother keeps the child;
- a child has a right to be brought up by his own parents;
- it exploits women.

The legal position

The practice of surrogacy raises many legal questions. What is the role of the law in relation to surrogacy? What is the legal status of surrogacy agreements? Should payments be allowed to the surrogate mother? How should the law deal with disputes over the child which is born? As regards the role of the law, the Warnock Report argued that private surrogacy arrangements should not be subject to legal control and, clearly, it would be impossible for the law to control such activity. But the Report was also keen to stop the commercial development of surrogacy.

The first case involving surrogacy was heard in 1978, although it did not appear in the law reports until some years later. In *A v C* (1985), Mr A and his partner, who could not have any more children, made an agreement with C that C would have a child using Mr A's sperm in return for £3,000. C refused to give up the baby. It was held at first instance that the agreement was unenforceable but Mr A could have access to the child. On appeal by C, the Court of Appeal described it as 'a bizarre and unnatural arrangement' and said that A should not have access to the child. In the later case of *Re C (A Minor) (Wardship: Surrogacy)* (1985), an American couple wanted a child and, as the woman was unable to bear children, they sought a surrogate mother through an agency. Kim Cotton, a mother in the UK, agreed to have a baby through artificial insemination with the commissioning father's sperm. The local council obtained a place of safety order for the child and the genetic father started wardship proceedings to obtain the child. The court considered that Kim Cotton had given up all rights to the baby and said that 'the moral, ethical and social considerations are for others and not for this court in its wardship jurisdiction'. The court focused on what was in the best interests of the child and said that the couple should look after it.

At the time that these cases were heard, the courts were clearly against the idea of surrogacy arrangements and their views reflected the public view. The Government's response was to pass the Surrogacy

Arrangements Act 1985. The aim of the Act is to prevent agencies from making money from surrogacy arrangements. Under s 2(1), it is an offence to: (a) initiate or take part in negotiations with a view to making a surrogacy arrangement; (b) offer or agree to negotiate the making of a surrogacy arrangement; or (c) collect information to use in making a surrogacy arrangement. But it is not an offence for anyone who wishes to be a surrogate mother to do the above acts (s 2(2)) or receive payment (s 2(3)). Similarly, someone wishing to be a commissioning parent does not commit an offence in these circumstances and may make payments to the surrogate mother. But one effect of s 2 is that doctors and lawyers could not be paid for any help or advice they would give in such matters, for example, a lawyer who draws up a surrogacy agreement.

Under s 3, it is an offence to advertise for or as a surrogate mother. But, under s 3(2), if a woman advertises to be a surrogate mother, she does not commit an offence unless she is the proprietor, editor or publisher of the newspaper containing the advertisement.

The Surrogacy Arrangements Act 1985 was amended by the HFEA 1990, s 36(1) of which added a new s 1A to the Surrogacy Arrangements Act 1985 and made all surrogacy arrangements unenforceable. The new s 1A provides, 'No surrogacy arrangement is enforceable by or against any of the persons making it'. However, private surrogacy arrangements are not illegal and there is, therefore, an ambivalence in the law. In the US case of *Re Baby M* (1987), the court had to consider an agreement under which a surrogate mother consented to artificial insemination with the sperm of a husband and agreed to give the baby to the husband and his wife. It was also agreed that the surrogate mother would be paid $10,000 and that the wife would adopt the child. When the baby was born, the surrogate mother refused to give up the child. The court said at first instance that the contract was valid and had been broken. But the Supreme Court of New Jersey said that the contract was invalid, as it broke laws forbidding payment for adoption and the adoption of the child was void. It was also against public policy for the surrogate mother to give up all rights to the child. However, as the baby had lived with the husband and wife for 18 months, the court allowed it to remain with them.

The English courts have had similar difficulties in dealing with surrogacy agreements. In *Re P (Minors) (Wardship: Surrogacy)* (1987), a divorced woman, Mrs P, made an agreement to have a child for Mr and Mrs B, in return for payment. Twins were born and Mrs P refused to hand them over. The court said that the welfare of the children was the important factor. In deciding on this matter, the court looked at the two families the twins could end up with. One family, Mr and Mrs B, had two parents, was better off financially and provided a more stimulating environment. But the other family had their natural mother, Mrs P, with whom they had bonded over a period of five months. The court had to carry out a balancing exercise and awarded care of the twins to the mother.

A novel situation arose in December 1999, when a homosexual couple, Barry Drewitt and Tony Barlow, had twins using the sperm of one of them and eggs from a woman donor, which were carried by a surrogate mother. The twins were born in California and the two men were registered as the parents. In English law, the surrogate mother is the legal mother and her husband is the legal father. The question arose as to whether they could be admitted to the UK, as the twins were not British citizens. They were allowed into the country, as this was considered to be more in their best interests than returning to their surrogate mother. The homosexual couple cannot apply for a parental order under s 30 of the 1990 Act, because they are not parties to a marriage. The outcome of proceedings is awaited.

It would seem that the commissioning couple are at a disadvantage compared to the mother in gaining control of the child. However, the mother in both of the above cases has been the genetic mother, that is, there is a partial surrogacy. If the commissioning couple provide the embryo, so that the surrogate mother merely carries the child (full surrogacy), the couple may have a stronger claim, although, legally, under s 27(1) of the 1990 Act, the surrogate mother is the legal mother in both cases.

Who are the legal parents of a child born to a surrogate mother?

At common law, a woman who gives birth to a child is the mother and, if she is married, her husband is presumed to be the father. If the woman is not married, then she has parental responsibility under s 2(2) of the Children Act 1989 but the father does not have parental responsibility. However, the father can acquire parental responsibility by making an agreement with the mother that he should have parental responsibility, or parental responsibility may be granted to a father by the court (s 4 of the Children Act 1989). These rules have caused problems when applied in cases of assisted reproduction. For example, if an embryo is placed in an infertile woman who gives birth to a child, she is the mother, even though she is not genetically related to the child. In *Re W (Minors) (Surrogacy)* (1991), a married woman agreed to be implanted with an embryo created *in vitro* from the commissioning father's sperm and commissioning mother's egg. The surrogate mother agreed to hand over the child, which she did at birth. In law, the surrogate mother was treated as the mother and her husband would be treated as the father if he had agreed to the procedure.

In the light of this case, a new section (s 30) was added to the HFEA 1990, which was at that time going through Parliament. Under s 30(1), the court may make an order (parental order) for a child to be treated as the child of a commissioning couple who are married, if the child has been carried by another woman as the result of the placing in her of an embryo or sperm and eggs or her artificial insemination and the gametes of one or both of the commissioning couple were used to create the embryo. Certain conditions, set out in sub-ss 2–7, must be met:

(2) the application must be made within six months of the birth;

(3) at the time of the application the child's home is with the husband and wife;

(4) the husband and wife are both over 18 years;

(5) the father of the child, (if he is not the husband) and the woman who carried the child have agreed to the making of the order;

(6) in (5) no agreement is needed if the person cannot be found and the woman's agreement is not valid if given under six weeks from the child's birth;

(7) no money or other benefit, other than for reasonable expenses, has been given or received by the husband and wife in relation to the making of the order unless authorised by a court.

This section restricts obtaining a parental order to heterosexual married couples and has been widely criticised as discriminatory against others who may wish to have such rights. In *Re Q* (1996), an unmarried surrogate mother gave birth to a child created from the egg of the wife and donated sperm provided through a licensed clinic. The commissioning couple applied for a parental order under s 30 of the 1990 Act and the question arose as to who was the father for the purpose of giving consent. It was held that, under s 28(6) of the Act, a man who donated sperm for the purpose of licensed treatment was not to be treated as the father of the child. If the surrogate mother had been married, the embryo had not been created with her husband's sperm and he had consented to the procedure, he would have been treated as the father under s 28(2). This did not apply, so, under s 28(3), if the embryo was placed in the woman or she was artificially inseminated, if the course of treatment provided for 'her and a man together' by a licensed clinic and the embryo was not created using the sperm of that man, that man should be treated as the father. But this did not apply here, as the section envisaged medical treatment for the man. The result was that there was no man who could be treated as the father and whose consent was necessary.

When an application is made under s 30 of the HFEA 1990, the court must be satisfied that no money or other benefit, other than reasonable expenses, has been given or received by the commissioning parents.

Future developments

The history of surrogacy shows that, initially, there was widespread antipathy to the practice, both from the general public and the legal and medical professions. In *A v C* (1985), a surrogacy arrangement was described as 'most extraordinary and irresponsible'. The impact of the Warnock Report and the Surrogacy Arrangements Act 1985 was to stop the development of commercial agencies for surrogacy, and, although private surrogacy was not banned, it was not encouraged. Over time, attitudes have changed and a more liberal view has been taken. The British Medical Association (BMA), in *Conceptions of Motherhood: The Practice of Surrogacy in Britain* (1996) shows an acceptance of the practice in focusing on the welfare of both the baby born and the surrogate mother, although the BMA considers that surrogacy is a 'last resort' for infertile women. There has also been the establishment of organisations which operate on a non-commercial basis to help those wishing to have children through surrogacy or to be surrogate mothers, for example, Childlessness Overcome Through Surrogacy (COTS).

In 1998, a Committee under the chairmanship of Professor Margaret Brazier produced its Report, *Surrogacy: Review for Health Ministers of Current Arrangements for Payments and Regulation* (Cm 4068). The Committee considered whether payments should be made to surrogate mothers, whether surrogacy arrangements should be regulated and whether any changes were required as a result to the

Surrogacy Arrangements Act 1985 and the HFEA 1990. The Committee made the following recommendations:

(a) Payments: payments to surrogate mothers should cover only genuine expenses associated with the pregnancy; further payments should be prohibited to stop such arrangements from being made for money; legislation should define expenses in broad terms of principle, leaving details to be given through regulations.

(b) Regulation: agencies involved in surrogacy arrangements should be registered with the Department of Health, which should draw up a Code of Practice.

(c) Legislation: the Surrogacy Arrangements Act 1985 and s 30 of the HFEA 1990 should be repealed and replaced by a new Surrogacy Act, which should set out the main legal principles governing surrogacy arrangements. These would include the following:

- surrogacy contracts should be non-enforceable;
- prohibition of commercial agencies;
- new statutory provisions in relation to payments to surrogate mothers;
- a Code of Practice;
- registration of non-profit making surrogacy agencies;
- prohibition of unregistered agencies;
- a revised s 30 parental order, under which applicants must prove that they have followed the Surrogacy Act. Further parental orders should only be available in the High Court and the commissioning couple must be resident in the UK, Channel Islands or the Isle of Man.

These recommendations seek to bring all the rules into one Act of Parliament and to make improvements as regards payment and regulation. The Brazier Committee saw surrogacy as a special and distinct form of fertility treatment, requiring its own special regulations, under which the welfare of the child must be paramount. This was because a woman was carrying a child who was given to others and all parties in the process were vulnerable. As a step forward, the Committee suggested that, as an interim measure, a voluntary code should be drawn up.

The Human Rights Act 1998

The Articles likely to be useful in this area are Arts 12 and 8. Article 12 provides that 'Men and women of marriageable age have the right to marry and to found a family, according to the national laws governing the exercise of this right'. This Article has been held to apply only to opposite sexes and, in *Cossey v UK* (1990), a man who had had a sex change was not allowed to marry. By analogy, the right to found a family would be similarly limited. Article 8(1) provides that 'Everyone has the right to respect for his private and family life'. This is subject to the qualification in Art 8(2):

> There shall be no interference by a public authority with the exercise of this right except as is in accordance with the law and is necessary in a democratic society in the interests of national security, public safety or the economic well-being of the country, for the prevention of disorder or crime, for the protection of health or morals, or for the protection of the rights and freedoms of others.

It has been held that the right to family life does not include life with a transsexual partner (*X, Y and Z v UK* (1997)) but this may be within private life. However, challenges may be made to widen the scope of family life to include same sex partners and bring them within the scope of Art 8. In *X, Y and Z v UK*, X was a female to male transsexual, who had lived with a woman, Y, for some years. In 1992, Y gave birth to Z, who had been conceived through artificial insemination by donor. X was refused permission to be registered as the father of Z. X, Y and Z claimed that the refusal to register X as Z's father was an infringement of their right to respect for family life under Art 8 of the European Convention on Human Rights. The European Court of Human Rights said that the issue was the relationship between a child conceived by AID and the person who had the role of the father, and how the law should treat them. There was no general agreement between States on such issues and the UK was not in breach of Art 8 by not recognising X as Z's father.

7 Abortion

You should be familiar with the following areas:

- offences under: OAPA 1861; Infant Life (Preservation) Act 1929
- circumstances in which abortion is allowed under s 1(1)(a)–(d) of the Abortion Act 1967
- requirements of Abortion Act as to who should carry out abortions and participation
- rights of: pregnant woman; foetus; father
- liability for injuries in relation to birth
- claims for wrongful life; wrongful birth

Introduction

Abortion means ending a pregnancy by destroying the foetus. There were approximately 170,000 abortions performed in 1999. The issue of abortion raises some of the most profound questions in medical law and ethics. When does human life begin? When does a 'person' come into existence? Does a foetus have a right to life? Does a woman have the right to do what she wants with her own body? The debate on abortion has polarised between those who claim that the foetus has a right to life (pro-life) and those who argue that a woman has the right to do what she wants with her own body (right to choose). A deontological (duty) approach would argue that there is a duty to maintain life (sanctity of life) and would not allow abortions. The utilitarian view would consider whether the consequences of having abortions were better for the overall good of society than not having them, with no particular concern for the foetus. Many of the issues cannot be solved and the law often has to take a pragmatic line, at the risk of pleasing neither side.

Development of the law on abortion

Abortion was a misdemeanour at common law. Various Acts of Parliament were passed in the 19th century which made abortion a criminal offence, culminating in the Offences Against the Person Act (OAPA) 1861. Section 58 of this Act provides that it is an offence for a pregnant woman to give herself poison or to unlawfully use an instrument or other means with intent to procure a miscarriage. The section also provides that anyone else who unlawfully gives a woman poison or unlawfully uses an instrument to procure a miscarriage commits an offence. In the case of someone, apart from the woman herself, carrying out the act, they may be convicted, whether the woman is pregnant or not, but they must have had a belief that she was pregnant (*R v Price* (1968)). Section 59 provides that it is an offence to supply poison or instruments in the knowledge that they will be used to procure the miscarriage of a woman, whether she is pregnant or not. Glanville Williams, in his *Textbook of Criminal Law* (3rd edn, 1996, Stevens), notes that it would be extremely unlikely for a woman to be prosecuted for procuring an abortion on herself because it would be something done in distress and she would be likely to injure herself in doing so.

The OAPA 1861 protected the foetus *in utero* and, once the child was born, it was protected by the law of homicide. However, while the baby was being born, it was not protected by the law. The Infant Life (Preservation) Act (IL(P)A) 1929 was passed to fill this gap in the law. Section 1 provides:

(1) ... any person who, with intent to destroy the life of a child capable of being born alive, by any wilful act causes a child to die before it has an existence independent of its mother, shall be guilty of felony, to wit, of child destruction ... Provided that no person shall be found guilty of an offence under this section unless it is proved that the act which caused the death of the child was not done in good faith for the purpose only of preserving the life of the mother.

(2) For the purposes of this Act, evidence that a woman had at any material time been pregnant for a period of 28 weeks or more shall be *prima facie* proof that she was at that time pregnant of a child capable of being born alive.

The IL(P)A 1929 therefore creates the offence of child destruction. The Act applies to any child 'capable of being born alive' and this covers any child, from 28 weeks' gestation onwards. There is some overlap with the OAPA 1861, which protects the foetus up until the start of birth. It is not an offence if the foetus is killed in the course of saving the mother's life. This defence was included because, before the development of Caesarean operations, if normal delivery of the foetus was not possible, the doctor would have to crush the skull of the foetus to save the mother's life. The OAPA 1861 did not have this defence and the question was whether a doctor who ended a pregnancy before the 28 week point was guilty of an offence under the OAPA 1861.

In *R v Bourne* (1938), a 14 year old girl became pregnant after being raped and the defendant doctor carried out an abortion with the consent of her parents. He was charged with procuring a miscarriage under s 58 of the OAPA 1861. The court said that the word 'unlawfully' as regards the use of any instrument to procure a miscarriage was not meaningless, but could be given the meaning found in s 1(1) of the IL(P)A 1929. The court then considered the phrase 'for the purpose of preserving the life of the mother' in s 1(1) and said that it included both the physical and mental health of the mother. Here, the girl's life was not in danger but her mental health was. The court said that the burden of proof was on the prosecution to prove that the defendant had not carried out the abortion in good faith to preserve the life of the mother. The jury acquitted the defendant.

Modern methods of contraception

Some methods of contraception, such as the 'morning after pill' and the intra-uterine device (coil), could be seen as causing an abortion if they take effect after fertilisation. If this is the case, then the requirements of the Abortion Act 1967 (see below) would have to be met. But it is generally accepted that anything done before implantation is legal and does not come within the phrase 'to procure a miscarriage' under the OAPA 1861. If a method of contraception does affect the foetus after implantation, a prosecution could be made under the 1861 Act.

The Abortion Act 1967

The Abortion Act 1967 provided that abortion would be legal if carried out under certain conditions. One of the reasons behind the Act was to end the practice of 'back street' abortions, which often caused injury to women. The Abortion Act 1967 was amended by the Human Fertilisation and Embryology Act 1990, s 1(1) of which provides that a registered medical practitioner (doctor) may terminate a pregnancy if two doctors are of the opinion that one of the grounds specified in the Act are complied with:

(a) the pregnancy has not exceeded 24 weeks and continuing it would involve greater risk to the physical or mental health of the pregnant woman or her existing children than if the pregnancy was ended; or

(b) termination is necessary to prevent grave permanent injury to the physical or mental health of the pregnant woman; or

(c) continuing the pregnancy would involve greater risk to the life of the pregnant woman that ending it; or

(d) there is a substantial risk that, if the child were born, it would suffer such physical or mental abnormalities that it would be seriously handicapped.

Section 1(2) provides that, in determining the risk to health in paras (a) and (b), the pregnant woman's 'actual or reasonably foreseeable environment' may be taken into account.

Ground (a) is often known as the 'social' ground for abortion, because the effect of s 1(2) is to allow such matters as home and family circumstances to be considered. The risk to the woman of continuing the pregnancy until birth must be greater that ending the pregnancy by having an abortion. Abortions in the first 12 weeks of pregnancy are a lesser risk than continuing the pregnancy, so there is no problem with such early terminations. The doctor has to make a decision that, on balance, termination has less risk than continuing the pregnancy. This ground covers risk to the mother's health and the health of her existing children. It may also be argued that this ground would cover having an abortion because the foetus is female, as in Asian cultures, where male children are favoured and female children are seen as a burden. Having a female baby could, therefore, affect the mental health of the mother.

The 24 week time limit is, in practice, measured from the first day of the woman's last period.

Ground (b) allows an abortion to prevent grave permanent injury to the pregnant woman. There is no time limit for this ground. Also, s 1(4) provides that one doctor who forms the opinion, in good faith, that termination is immediately necessary to prevent grave permanent injury may authorise the abortion.

Abortion is allowed under ground (c) only if the risk to the life of the pregnant woman by continuing with the pregnancy is greater than terminating the pregnancy. There is no time limit under this ground. Again, s 1(4) allows one doctor to authorise an abortion.

Ground (d) allows an abortion if two doctors believe, in good faith, that there is a substantial risk that, if a child was born, it would suffer such physical or mental abnormalities as to be seriously handicapped. The Act does not define what is meant by 'seriously handicapped' and this could allow a wide interpretation, leading to abortion for relatively minor handicaps, for example, if the foetus had a withered hand. Another difficulty with the interpretation of this ground is the matter of whether the handicap has to exist when the child is born or at some later point.

There is still argument over whether the Abortion Act 1967 gives a right to 'abortion on demand', as the vast majority are carried out under s 1(1)(a) – the 'social' ground. However, a woman seeking an abortion on the NHS, rather than privately, is dependent on finding a doctor to agree and there is wide variation in practice within the NHS. If a doctor keeps within the rules laid down in the Act, there seems to be a wide scope for allowing abortions.

Incompetent patients

An incompetent adult or a child cannot consent to an abortion. If a child is 'Gillick competent', they could consent to an abortion. In the case of an incompetent adult, an abortion could be performed in her best interests. If there is a conflict between a Gillick competent child and their parents, the matter would have to decided by a court.

The Abortion Act 1967 in practice

Section 1(1) of the Abortion Act 1967 provides that the termination should be carried out by a 'registered medical practitioner'. Originally, abortions were carried out surgically, by a doctor, but new methods enabled abortions to be carried out using drugs which caused the foetus to be expelled from the mother. It was usually nurses who administered the drugs. The Department of Health and Social Security (DHSS) issued a circular which stated that nurses who terminated a pregnancy by such a method committed no offence under the

Abortion Act 1967. In *Royal College of Nursing v DHSS* (1981), the House of Lords considered the issue. They held that the interpretation of the phrase had to be seen in the light of the purpose of the Act – that abortions should be carried out with proper skill. This particular process was authorised by a doctor and was carried out under the supervision of a doctor; therefore, it fell within the provisions of the Act. On the question of whether the procedure was carried out by a registered medical practitioner, Lord Keith said:

> In my opinion, this question is to be answered affirmatively. The doctor has responsibility for the whole process and is in charge of it throughout. It is he who decides that it is to be carried out. He personally performs essential parts of it which are such as to necessitate the application of his particular skill. The nurse's actions are done under his direct written instructions. In the circumstances, I find it impossible to hold that the doctor's role is other than that of a principal, and I think he would be very surprised to hear that the nurse was the principal and he himself only an accessory.

However, the decision was by a narrow majority of 3:2 and Lord Wilberforce, in a dissenting judgment, said that allowing nurses to carry out the procedure was extending the law, a task which should be left to Parliament.

The Abortion Act 1967 provides a 'conscientious objection' clause. Section 4 reads as follows:

(1) ... subject to subsection (2) of this section, no person shall be under any duty, whether by contract or by any other legal requirement, to participate in any treatment authorised by this Act to which he has a conscientious objection; provided that in any legal proceedings the burden of proof of conscientious objection shall rest on the person claiming to rely on it.

(2) Nothing in subsection (1) of this section shall affect any duty to participate in treatment which is necessary to save the life or prevent grave permanent injury to the physical or mental health of a pregnant woman.

Therefore, no person is under a duty to 'participate in any treatment' if they have a conscientious objection. And s 4(2) provides that the exception does not apply if there is an emergency and treatment is necessary to save the life or prevent grave permanent injury to the pregnant woman. If a doctor had to carry out an abortion in an emergency, he could not rely on the exception. In *Janaway v Salford HA* (1989), J, a Catholic who objected to abortion, was a medical secretary who was asked to type a letter referring a patient for the termination of a pregnancy. She refused to do this on the ground of conscientious objection and was subsequently dismissed. She brought a claim for unfair dismissal and argued that she could refuse to type the letter under s 4(1) of the Abortion Act, as it was participating in treatment. The House of Lords held that the phrase 'participate in any treatment' meant the actual medical process of the abortion and J was not justified in refusing to type a letter.

This is quite a narrow interpretation of 'participate in any treatment' and means that administrative duties in connection with abortion or merely giving advice about abortion would not be covered by s 4.

Place of treatment

Section 1(3) provides that abortions must be carried out in an NHS hospital or other place approved by the Secretary of State. The object of this requirement was to ensure that abortions took place in suitable conditions. Section 1(3A) provides for other places to be approved in the case of medicines used to effect abortions. This covers the use of drugs such as RU486 (known as the abortion pill), which must be used in the first two months of pregnancy. RU486 effectively stops implantation of the fertilised ovum or causes it to be discharged and it is covered by the Abortion Act 1967, so the requirements of the Act must be met.

The rights of the foetus

An enduring problem in connection with abortion is trying to determine the moral status of the foetus and to decide when a foetus becomes a person. A wide range of suggestions have been made about what constitutes 'personhood'. Tooley has argued that self-awareness is necessary for personhood but this would exclude newborn babies. Kant, arguing from a deontological viewpoint, said that rational agents were persons. This is an even higher threshold and would exclude young children and some adults. Ronald Dworkin has said that, from conception, the foetus is a form of human life. The Catholic Church's position is that a human being is created from the moment of conception. Suggestions for the exact point at which personhood occurs include conception, implantation of the embryo, viability, birth, or some later point.

English law has considered the rights of the foetus in a number of cases. In *Paton v Trustees of BPAS* (1978), a wife wished to have an abortion and obtained the permission of two doctors without consulting her husband. The husband applied to the court for an injunction to stop the abortion. The High Court held that the husband had no rights under the Abortion Act 1967 to stop an abortion. Sir George Baker said: 'The foetus cannot, in English law, in my view, have any right of its own, at least until it is born and has a separate existence from the mother.' The husband took his case to the European Commission on Human Rights, claiming that the foetus had rights under Art 2 of the European Convention on Human Rights (the right to life), but this was rejected. The Commission said:

> If Article 2 were held to cover the foetus and its protection under this Article were, in the absence of any express limitation, seen as absolute, an abortion would have to be considered as prohibited even where the continuance of the pregnancy would involve a serious risk to the life of the pregnant woman. This would mean that the 'unborn life' of the foetus would be regarded as being of a higher value than the life of the pregnant woman.

The Court of Appeal also considered the issue in *Re F (In Utero)* (1988). A mother who had a history of mental illness and drug abuse and had led a nomadic existence around Europe, was 38 weeks pregnant when she disappeared from her flat. The local authority wished to make the unborn child a ward of court. The court held that it did not have jurisdiction and said that it is the interests of the child which are predominant, but this would cause a conflict with the interests of the mother. This, in turn, would lead to difficulties if an order was made against the mother and she refused to comply with it. Only minors can be made wards of court and a minor can only be a person if they have been born. In *St George's Healthcare NHS Trust v S* (1998), the court said that 'an unborn child is not a separate person from its mother. Its need for medical assistance does not prevail over her rights'. The court went on to say that a pregnant woman could refuse treatment even though her own life and that of her unborn child depended on it.

In *AG's Reference (No 3 of 1994)* (1998), the defendant stabbed his pregnant girlfriend in the stomach. A baby was born but died three months later from injuries caused by the stabbing. The House of Lords said that a conviction for constructive manslaughter would be possible. The House of Lords rejected the argument of the Court of Appeal that the foetus should be treated as an integral part of the mother. Lord Mustill stated that:

The mother's leg was part of the mother; the foetus was not ... I would, therefore, reject the reasoning which assumes that, since (in the eyes of English law) the foetus does not have the attributes which make it a 'person', it must be an adjunct of the mother. Eschewing all religious and political debate, I would say that the foetus is neither. It is a unique organism.

The rights of the pregnant woman

The Abortion Act 1967 does not give the pregnant woman a legal right to demand an abortion. Montgomery (*Health Care Law*, 1997, OUP) says that doctors control access to abortions and this varies widely throughout the country. In the US, the Supreme Court in *Roe v Wade* (1973) said that the constitutional right to privacy in the US Constitution included a woman's right to abortion up to the time that the foetus was viable. After this, the State had a right to intervene on behalf of the foetus, unless the life or health of the mother was threatened.

There is growing awareness of the fact that tobacco, alcohol and drugs which are taken by the mother can have an effect on the unborn baby. But can, or should, the actions of the mother be controlled? The Law Commission has said that the foetus should not have a right of action against the mother, as this would compromise the mother-child relationship. In the Canadian case of *Winnipeg Child and Family Services (Northwest Area) v G* (1997), the mother, a glue sniffing addict, was five months pregnant and the court ordered that the mother should be detained to protect the unborn child. The Supreme Court set this judgment aside and said that the foetus' existence was dependent on the body of the woman and any intervention on behalf of the foetus could conflict with the mother's interests. It was not appropriate for a court to extend the law in such a way.

This conflict between mother and foetus is also seen in cases where the mother refuses medical treatment which could lead to harm to the foetus. In the US case of *Re AC* (1987), a woman who was 26 weeks pregnant was dying of cancer but refused a Caesarean section. The court ordered the operation to be carried out but both the baby and the mother died two days later. An appeal court later reversed the decision and said that a decision of a competent patient should prevail, unless there are compelling reasons to override it. The English courts have dealt with numerous cases involving this conflict between a pregnant woman and her foetus. In *Re S (Adult: Refusal of Medical Treatment)* (1992), the pregnant woman refused a Caesarean section on religious grounds but the court granted a declaration allowing the operation to save the life of the mother and the child.

In *Re MB (Medical Treatment)* (1997), the woman was 40 weeks pregnant and the foetus was in the breach position; natural delivery would risk brain damage or death to the child. The mother agreed to a Caesarean section but, due to a fear of needles, refused the anaesthetic. The local health authority applied for a declaration that treatment would be lawful. It was held by the Court of Appeal, in overruling *Re S* (1992), that a competent woman may refuse treatment for any reason or no reason, even though the consequences may be death or serious handicap for the child or her own death. The court said that the woman was temporally incompetent and allowed the Caesarean section. In *St George's NHS Trust v S* (1998), the Court of Appeal said that an unborn child's need for medical assistance does not prevail over the rights of the mother: 'She is entitled not to be forced to submit to an invasion of her body against her will, whether her own life or that of her unborn child depends on it.'

The rights of the father

The husband in *Paton v BPAS* (1979) had claimed an injunction to stop the mother from having an abortion. The court considered the fact that the provisions of the Abortion Act 1967 had been complied with and said: 'The husband, therefore, in my view, has no legal right enforceable at law or in equity to stop his wife having this abortion ...' The father then took the case to the European Commission on Human Rights in *Paton v UK* (1980), arguing that his right under Art 8 of the European Convention on Human Rights, the right to respect for family life, had been broken. The Commission, in applying Art 8(2) ('There shall be no interference by a public authority with the exercise of this right except such as is in accordance with the law and is necessary ... for the protection of the rights and freedoms of others') said that, here, the rights of the mother had to be protected and dismissed his claim. Later, in *C v S* (1998), the Court of Appeal confirmed that a father had no right to stop an abortion. In the Scottish case of *Kelly v Kelly* (1997), the court held that a father could not stop his wife from having an abortion. Although a father has responsibilities and rights after a child is born, before that time he has no rights.

Liability for injuries in relation to birth

If a foetus suffers an injury whilst it is in the womb (*in utero*) and, as a result, is born disabled, does it have a right of action against the person causing the injury? Under the Congenital Disabilities (Civil Liability) Act 1976, a child born after 21 July 1976 has a statutory right to claim damages. Under s 1, if a child is born disabled as a result of a negligent act before its birth, the child will have a claim. It must be proved that the negligent act affected:

- the ability of either parent to have a healthy child; or

- the mother during pregnancy; or

- the mother or child during birth,

and the child would not otherwise have been disabled.

Under s 4(1), the mother cannot be liable under the Act except for injuries caused to the foetus as a result of her negligent driving. This claim was allowed because the mother will have compulsory insurance against liability. The Law Commission said, before the Act was passed, that a claim should not be allowed by the child against the mother because of the effect this would have on the relationship between them. The child must be born alive to bring a claim (s 4(2)). The Act replaces the common law for those children born after the Act was passed (s 4(5)). The duty to the child is owed through the parent, so the defendant must be in breach of a duty owed to the parents (s 1(3)), although the parents do not have to suffer injury themselves.

The common law position on such a claim was unclear until *Burton v Islington HA* (1992). A pregnant woman had a routine operation but the hospital had not tested to see whether she was pregnant. As a result of the operation, the foetus was damaged. The child was born disabled in 1967. Obviously, this all happened before the 1976 Act. The defendant claimed that it was not liable, because, at the time of the operation, the claimant was not a living person and had no legal rights. The Court of Appeal held that a duty of care was owed to the foetus because it was foreseeable that the foetus could be damaged. If the child was born alive, this duty crystallised and the child could sue for negligence. However, since the Act was passed, the common law rules only apply to those born before the Act, as provided in s 4(5).

Claim for wrongful life

This is a claim that the child who is born disabled as a result of negligence would have been better off if they had not been born at all. This type of claim may arise, for example, if a hospital fails to tell a woman, before she becomes pregnant, that, because of a genetic defect, she may have a disabled child; or where a hospital negligently screens a pregnant woman and misses an abnormality in the foetus and, consequently, a disabled child is born. The claim is brought by the child.

In *McKay v Essex AHA* (1982), a pregnant woman suspected that she had German Measles and was given a blood test by the defendants. She was negligently told that she did not have the disease, continued with the pregnancy and the baby was born disabled in 1975. The Court of Appeal considered what the effect would be if the child's claim was allowed and said that it would be imposing a duty on doctors to carry out an abortion in all cases where abnormality was suspected:

> To impose such a duty towards the child would, in my opinion, make a further inroad on the sanctity of human life, which would be contrary to public policy. It would mean regarding the life of a handicapped child as not only less valuable than the life of a normal child, but so much less valuable that it was not worth preserving, and it would even mean that a doctor would be obliged to pay damages to a child infected with rubella before birth who was in fact born with some mercifully trivial abnormality. These are the consequences of the necessary basic assumption that a child has a right to be born whole or not at all, not to be born unless it can be born perfect or 'normal', whatever that may mean.

The court also said that it could not measure the loss to the child as the difference between its present condition and its condition if it had not been born, as a court of law could not evaluate non-existence. Therefore, the claim failed. Ackner LJ said that no claim for wrongful life could be made under the Congenital Disabilities (Civil Liability) Act 1976 because the Act dealt with claims for being born disabled as a result of negligence, and not claims that the child should not have been born.

Although a claim for wrongful life by a child will fail, the parents may claim for the extra expense of bringing up a disabled child.

Claim for wrongful birth

Originally, a claim for wrongful birth could be made if a healthy child was born as a result of negligence (also known as wrongful conception) or a handicapped child was born as a result of negligence. Claims could be made either in contract or negligence.

The courts have not been consistent in dealing with these cases and have varied their approaches between following legal principles and following public policy. What if a healthy child is born because of a negligently performed sterilisation or because the parents are not warned about the possibility of reversal of a sterilisation? In *Udale v Bloomsbury HA* (1983), the claimant became pregnant after a sterilisation was carried out negligently. She claimed damages for the pain of childbirth and the cost of bringing up the child. The court said that it would be 'highly undesirable' for a child to know that a court has declared his life a mistake; the mother's joy would cancel out the inconvenience and financial disadvantage of having a child; and, in our culture, a child is regarded as a blessing. The court said that it would be against public policy to award damages for the cost of bringing up the child and rejected that claim. However, damages were given for the pain and suffering of childbirth.

This case was followed by *Emeh v Kensington AHA* (1985), which also involved a negligently performed sterilisation which led to the birth of a child with congenital abnormalities. The Court of Appeal said that the courts should follow legal principle and rejecting such claims as a matter of policy was wrong. It was unreasonable to expect the woman to have an abortion and damages were awarded for the cost of bringing up the child. In *Thake v Maurice* (1986), the Thakes had five children and did not want any more. Mr Thake paid for a vasectomy operation and his wife later became pregnant after the vasectomy was naturally reversed. The Court of Appeal held that it was negligent not to warn of this risk. Mrs Thake did not realise she was pregnant until it was too late to have an abortion, but, if she had been warned, she would have been alert to the possibility and could have had an abortion. The court awarded damages for bringing up the child. In the High Court, Pain J had said, 'Every baby has a belly to be filled and a body to be clothed'.

More recently, the matter has been reviewed by the House of Lords in *McFarlane v Tayside Health Board* (2000). Mr M had a vasectomy and was later told that he could dispense with contraception. Mrs M then became pregnant and gave birth to their fifth child, a healthy baby. The parents claimed damages for the pain and suffering of childbirth and the cost of bringing up the child. The court said that, as a matter of principle, the parents of a healthy child which was born because of a failed sterilisation were not entitled to claim the cost of bringing up the child. It was not fair, just and reasonable to impose a duty on the doctor for the consequential responsibilities imposed on or accepted by the parents to bring up the child. As a matter of justice, the law did not allow the parents of a healthy but unwanted child to claim the cost of bringing it up. But the mother was entitled to damages for the pain and suffering of pregnancy and giving birth.

Following *McFarlane*, claims for wrongful conception and wrongful birth resulting in the birth of a healthy child will not succeed. The effect on claims for the birth of a handicapped child is uncertain. (See Maclean, A, *McFarlane v Tayside Health Board*: a wrongful conception in the House of Lords?' [2000] Web JCLI.)

If a claim is made because a handicapped child is born as a result of negligence by the hospital, the parents would have to establish that, if they had known the true facts, the mother would have had an abortion. This is necessary to establish causation because, if the mother would have continued with her pregnancy, then the hospital would not have caused the loss. In *Salih v Enfield HA* (1991), the defendants had negligently failed to warn the pregnant mother of the risk of rubella. The mother contracted the disease and, as a result, her child was born disabled. The Court of Appeal said that the parents were entitled to the cost of bringing up the child. But, in *Rand v East Dorset HA* (2000), which was decided after *McFarlane v Tayside Health Board*, Mrs Rand was not told that a scan taken during her pregnancy showed abnormalities and later she had a child with Down's syndrome. In a claim for wrongful birth, the claimants were awarded damages only for the loss arising as a result of the child's disability and not for the cost of bringing up the child.

The Human Rights Act 1998

Article 2 (the right to life) has been considered by the Court of Appeal in *Re F (In Utero)* (1988), where the court said that it could not be used to make the foetus a ward of court. In *Paton v UK* (1980), the European Court of Human Rights rejected the claim that a foetus had protection under Art 2.

8 Death

Introduction

Death is a taboo subject in contemporary society and it raises many difficult ethical and legal issues. Medical advances mean that more people can be kept alive for longer, and this merely highlights the problems. When does someone die? Is the principle of the sanctity of human life paramount and should all means be used to keep people alive, whatever the cost, or should there be limits on the use of scarce medical resources to keep people alive? Is there a right to life and a right to die? Are there legal and moral differences between killing and letting die? How should the criminal law deal with 'mercy killing'? There are also the difficult questions about the 'quality of life' of patients with terminal illnesses. What of the position of patients in a 'persistent vegetative state'; should treatment be withdrawn? How will the Human Rights Act 1998 affect the law in this area? This chapter will examine these issues. However, there are no simple resolutions to most of them.

Defining 'death'

Forty years ago, if someone's heart stopped, they would have been pronounced dead, but, fortunately, that is no longer the case, as it is now possible to resuscitate people. Deciding when someone is dead has changed over the years, as medical understanding and technology has advanced. In 1976, the Conference of Royal Colleges and their Faculties published a report that brain death could be diagnosed with certainty. It has been accepted by the medical profession that, if a patient is diagnosed as 'brain stem dead', this means that the patient is dead. Certain tests can be carried out to determine if this has happened and, once it is established, the process is irreversible, even though a patient may still be able to breathe using a ventilator. The courts have accepted this practice of the medical profession. In *R v Malcherek; R v Steel* (1981), M stabbed his wife, who was put on a ventilator. It was later discovered that she had irreversible brain damage and the ventilator was switched off. M argued that it was not him who had caused the death but the doctor, by switching off the ventilator. It was held by the Court of Appeal that the original act by M was a substantial and continuing cause of death. The doctor switching off the ventilator did not break the chain of causation, because the victim was already dead. The court did not give a definition of death but accepted the practice of doctors, who had concluded that the patient was, 'for all practical purposes', dead.

The courts confirmed in a later case that brain stem death means that someone is dead. In *Re A* (1992), a badly injured child was put on a ventilator but was later diagnosed as brain stem dead. The parents wanted the ventilator to be kept on. The court made a declaration that someone certified as brain stem dead was dead for all legal, as well as medical, purposes. If a doctor switched off the ventilator, the doctor was not acting illegally. The court added that the child could not be made a ward of court, as the court did not have jurisdiction over a dead child.

One problem with brain stem death is that it does not give a time of death; it tells us only that the patient is dead when the tests are carried out. This could cause problems in the law of succession if, for example, the exact time of death was important in determining who should inherit under a will.

The other issue is whether there should be a legal definition of 'death'. Those in favour of having a definition argue that this would bring certainty to the law, but the argument against is that any rigid definition would soon be out of date.

Knowledge that you are dying

Does a patient who is dying have the right to know that fact? In practice, doctors will frequently not tell a dying patient that they are dying. This may be justified on the basis that knowing might make the patient's condition worse. The patient will have access to their notes but the information they are dying may lawfully be withheld if it is likely to cause distress. However, the duty to respect the patient's autonomy would require a patient to be told whether they were dying, if the patient asked.

Suicide

Originally, suicide was a crime, but the Suicide Act 1961 changed the law and it is not now a criminal offence to take your own life. However, s 2(1) of that Act makes it an offence if someone 'aids, abets, counsels or procures the suicide of another, or an attempt by another to commit suicide'. In *AG v Able* (1984), the Voluntary Euthanasia Society distributed a leaflet setting out ways to commit suicide. The question arose as to whether this was an offence under s 2. Woolf J said that, in order to prove that distributing the booklet was assisting suicide under s 2(1), three things had to be proved: (a) that the defendant intended the booklet to be used by someone contemplating suicide; (b) that the defendant distributed the booklet to such a person; and (c) that such a person was assisted or encouraged to commit suicide by reading the booklet. It was held that the publication was not illegal, as the third requirement could not be proved in any particular case.

An offence may be committed under s 2 even if no attempt to commit suicide is made by the other person (*R v McShane* (1977)).

Is there a right to obtain help from a doctor to commit suicide? (This is called physician assisted suicide.) If a patient asked a doctor for a fatal dose of pills and the doctor handed over the pills, would that be an offence under s 2? It would seem to fall within s 2(1). It has been argued that patients should have the right to ask their doctor for help to commit suicide, as this would give the patient control over when they die.

In the US, in *Quill v Vacco* (1996), a court had ruled that a State law which made assisted suicide for the terminally ill a criminal offence was unconstitutional. It was argued that patients can ask for removal of life sustaining treatment, but those not on life sustaining treatment cannot obtain help to die and are therefore treated unequally, so physician assisted suicide should be made legal. The Supreme Court overruled this decision and said that there was a fundamental distinction between refusing treatment and actively ending life. This decision maintains the distinction between leaving a fatal does of pills for a patient and giving the patient a lethal injection.

Euthanasia

The word 'euthanasia' means bringing about a gentle and easy death. It is usually used in the context of killing someone with a terminal illness, who is in great pain. The idea of euthanasia has provoked a debate on whether it should be allowed by law. Those against euthanasia argue that the principle of the sanctity of life should be followed, which is based on the Christian principle that it is wrong to take a human life. However, the principle of the sanctity of life is not an absolute one and, in exceptional circumstances, it is permissible to kill, for example, in self-defence or war.

There are a number of ways in which euthanasia may be categorised:

(a) voluntary, involuntary and non-voluntary:

- voluntary – the patient asks for their life to be ended;
- involuntary – ending the patient's life without a request or against the patient's wishes;
- non-voluntary – ending the life of an incompetent patient who is unable to express their views;

(b) active and passive:

- active – a positive act to end the patient's life;
- passive – an omission which leads to the patient's death.

There is a long history of attempts to pass legislation which would make euthanasia lawful. In 1936, a Euthanasia Bill provided for someone over 21 who was suffering from an incurable illness to sign a form requesting euthanasia. This had to be witnessed by two people. A euthanasia referee would then interview the patient and, eventually, the case would go to court, which could authorise euthanasia. The Voluntary Euthanasia Bill 1969 allowed a patient over 21 years who was certified by two doctors as suffering from an incurable disease to request euthanasia in writing. Since that time, a number of other Bills have been introduced, but without success.

Active euthanasia

Active euthanasia, which is a deliberate act to end the life of the patient, is prohibited in English law and would lead to a charge of murder or manslaughter. In *R v Cox* (1992), an old lady who suffered from rheumatoid arthritis was in great pain and wanted to die. She asked Dr Cox to end her life. The doctor gave her an injection of potassium chloride, which is a poison and has no painkilling effects. She died a few minutes later. Dr Cox was convicted of attempted murder. The judge said: '... if he injected her with potassium chloride for the primary purpose of killing her, of hastening her death, he is guilty of the offence charged ...' The doctor's motive of helping to put the patient out of her misery was immaterial. It was unclear, on the evidence, whether the patient was so close to death that she would have died anyway. Dr Cox was given a sentence of one year's imprisonment, suspended for 12 months.

There is an exception to the above rule that a doctor cannot do an act which ends the life of a patient. This involves the ethical principle of 'double effect'. This principle says that a person can do an act which has a good objective if the *intention* is to produce the good objective but *in fact* it has a bad effect. There must be a sufficient reason to risk the bad effect. An example of how this might work is if a doctor gave a terminally ill patient, who was in great pain, an injection of painkilling drugs but these had the side effect of shortening the patient's life. In *R v Adams* (1957), Dr Adams gave large doses of morphine to an elderly patient who had suffered a stroke and, as a result of these injections, she died. Devlin J said:

> ... a doctor who was aiding the sick and dying need not calculate in minutes, or even hours, and perhaps not in days or weeks, the effect upon a patient's life of the medicines which he administers or else be in peril of a charge of murder. If the first purpose of medicine, the restoration of health, can no longer be achieved, there is still much for a doctor to do, and he is entitled to do all that is proper and necessary to relieve pain and suffering, even if the measures he takes may incidentally shorten life.

Dr Adams argued that he had given these doses to relieve pain and that shortening the patient's life was merely incidental to this purpose. He was found not guilty. In 1999, Dr David Moor injected a patient with a lethal amount of diamorphine but was found not guilty of murder. He argued that he gave the drug to ease pain:

> The family of the victim did not want Dr Moor to be prosecuted. In fact, Dr Moor had admitted to killing over 300 patients in this way and such practice is not uncommon amongst general practitioners. If doctors were allowed to kill patients, this would have a profound effect, not only on the role of the doctor, but also on the view taken of doctors by patients. Doctors would not then be viewed as healers.

Outline of euthanasia in The Netherlands

Active euthanasia is, strictly, a criminal offence in The Netherlands. Article 293 of the Dutch Criminal Code provides: 'Anyone who takes the life of another at that person's express and serious request, will be punished with a prison sentence.' In addition, helping someone to commit suicide is also a crime, as provided by Art 294. However, a doctor may claim the defence of necessity (or *force majeure*) under Art 40 if they act in the face of conflicting duties. In 1984, the Royal Dutch Medical Association set out guidelines which must be followed before euthanasia is carried out, and these were subsequently confirmed by the courts. The guidelines provide as follows:

* the patient must make a voluntary request;
* the request must be well considered and persistent;
* the patient must be in intolerable suffering (not necessarily physical);
* euthanasia must be a last resort;
* euthanasia must be performed by a doctor;
* the doctor must have consulted with an independent doctor.

In addition, the doctor must follow the procedure which was agreed by the Royal Dutch Medical Association and the Ministry of Justice in 1990. The doctor carrying out euthanasia must tell the local medical examiner that he is doing so; the examiner reports to the district attorney; and the attorney decides whether or not to prosecute. Doctors who follow the above guidelines and procedure are unlikely to be prosecuted. In the *Alkmaar* case (1985), a doctor was prosecuted under Art 293 after giving lethal injections to a 95 year old patient who was seriously ill and had no prospects of recovery. The patient had said she wanted to die. The Supreme Court held that the defence of necessity or *force majeure* under Art 40 could apply where there were conflicting duties, which were, in this case, to uphold the law against taking life and to act in the patient's best interests. It was considered that the doctor had acted in accordance with medical standards and he was acquitted. This case was widely seen as confirming the acceptability of active voluntary euthanasia if the guidelines were followed. In the later case of *Chabot* (1992), a depressed patient who had unsuccessfully attempted suicide (but who was not suffering from any other illnesses) consulted Dr Chabot for therapy. After one month, the patient still wanted to die and Dr Chabot provided her with a lethal dose, which she took in his presence. He was prosecuted under Art 294. The Supreme Court accepted that euthanasia was available to a patient with a psychiatric illness and that the defence of necessity was available to a doctor in such cases. But Dr Chabot was found guilty, because, although he had consulted seven other doctors, none of them had examined the patient, so there was no other evidence the doctor had acted in an emergency. However, no punishment was given because of the circumstances and the evidence that it was likely that the patient would have committed suicide anyway. This decision was seen as widening the availability of euthanasia and a step down a slippery slope.

A study of the practice of euthanasia in The Netherlands, the Remmelink Report (1991), reported that, in 1990, there were 2,300 cases of active voluntary euthanasia and 400 cases of assisted suicide (about 2% of all deaths). Although this could be seen as dispelling fears that thousands of patients were being killed, the number of cases not reported is unknown. A more recent study of euthanasia in The Netherlands concluded: 'The reality is that a clear majority of cases of euthanasia, both with or without consent, go unreported and unchecked. Dutch claims of effective regulation ring hollow.' (Keown, J and Jochensen, H, *Pro Life Infonet*, 1999, Amsterdam Legalise.) In 1999, legislation was proposed to legalise euthanasia. The reality is that euthanasia is practised in The Netherlands and this is accepted by the courts if the guidelines are followed.

The Dutch Parliament have recently passed legislation giving doctors immunity from prosecution for mercy killing and assisted suicide if they follow certain conditions ('Dutch become first to legalise euthanasia' (2000) *The Times*, 29 November). The article states that Dutch doctors already perform euthanasia on 3,200 patients each year.

Passive euthanasia

This is the ending of life by an omission to act. In fact, it covers situations of non-treatment, withdrawal of treatment and refusal of treatment. The legal position can be summed up in the words of the writer Arthur Clough: 'Thou shalt not kill but needs't not strive officiously to keep alive.' The law recognises a distinction between an act and an omission. But, in the context of medical care, health staff owe a duty to the patient and an omission to act to help the patient would be a breach of that duty. A layperson may also be under a duty to act to help another close relative. In *R v Stone and Dobinson* (1977), the defendants – a man aged 67 years, of low intelligence, and his mistress, who was mentally inadequate – took Stone's sister into their home. The sister was in her 50s. The sister developed anorexia nervosa and became bedridden. The defendants did not call a doctor to see her or obtain any other outside help. A month after taking to her bed, she was found dead as a result of blood poisoning from infected bed sores. It was held by the Court of Appeal that the defendants had taken on the duty of caring for the sister and were grossly negligent in failing to carry out that duty. They were convicted of manslaughter.

But is this distinction between acts and omissions always clear? If a doctor switches off the ventilator of a patient who has no chance of recovery, is this an act? In *Airedale NHS Trust v Bland* (1993), Lord Goff gave the example of a doctor switching off a machine as compared to an interloper who maliciously switches it off and stated that 'the doctor, in discontinuing life support, is simply allowing his patient to die of his pre-existing condition; the interloper is actively intervening to stop the doctor from prolonging the patient's life, and such conduct cannot possibly be categorised as an omission'. Mason and McCall-Smith point out that categorising switching off a machine as an omission is 'untenable'.

Even if a distinction can be made legally between killing and letting die, can the distinction be justified from an ethical standpoint? It may be argued that both the intention and the consequences of an act and an omission are the same and, therefore, there is no moral difference between them. In *Bland*, Lord Browne-Wilkinson commented:

> How can it be lawful to allow a patient to die slowly, though painlessly, over a period of weeks from lack of food but unlawful to produce his immediate death by a lethal injection, thereby saving his family from yet another ordeal to add to the tragedy that has already struck them? I find it difficult to find a moral answer to that question. But it is undoubtedly the law ...

Non-treatment

In some medical situations, medical staff follow a policy of non-treatment. Examples include certain new born babies and incompetent adults. The issue of non-treatment involves considering the question of the extent of the duty to act to save someone's life. The Catholic doctrine of ordinary and extraordinary means is relevant here. This doctrine was set out in a directive issued by Pope Pius XII in 1957:

> Man has a right and a duty in case of severe illness to take the necessary steps to preserve life and health ... But he is obliged at all times to employ only ordinary means ... that is to say those means which do not impose an extraordinary burden on himself or others.

The Pope added that 'ordinary' means depended on the 'circumstances of persons, places, times and cultures'. In applying this doctrine, it is not simply a question of deciding whether a proposed treatment is ordinary or extraordinary and, if it is ordinary, it must be given. It must also be considered whether the burden of the treatment would be too much or out of proportion to the benefit.

The common thread in cases of non-treatment is that treatment is futile or is not in the patient's best interests. In *R v Arthur* (1981), a baby was born with Down's syndrome but was otherwise healthy. The parents rejected the baby and Dr Arthur wrote in the notes, 'Parents do not wish it to survive, nursing care only'. Dr Arthur gave the baby an injection of a painkilling drug, which also had the effect of suppressing its appetite. The baby died three days later. Dr Arthur was initially charged with murder but this was reduced to attempted murder. The judge asked the jury to consider whether Dr Arthur was merely carrying out a holding operation or whether he had done a positive act to kill the baby. Dr Arthur was found not guilty by the jury. This case was followed by *Re B (A Minor) (Wardship: Medical Treatment)* (1981), where a baby was born with Down's syndrome and had a blockage of the intestine which could be treated. The parents refused to consent to treatment, even though, without it, the baby would die. The baby was made a ward of court. The Court of Appeal said that the baby should be given the chance to live and authorised the operation. The court had to consider the wishes of the parents and the doctors but, ultimately, it had to make a decision which was in the best interests of the child. Templeman LJ said:

> There may be cases, I know not, of severe proved damage where the future is so certain and where the life of the child is so bound to be full

of pain and suffering that the court might be driven to a different conclusion, but in the present case the choice which lies before the court is this: whether to allow an operation to take place which may result in the child living for 20 or 30 years as a mongoloid or whether (and I think this must be brutally the result) to terminate the life of a mongoloid child because she also has an intestinal complaint. Faced with that choice I have no doubt that it is the duty of this court to decide that the child must live.

These two cases seem to contradict each other, but it is likely that *Re B* will be followed and that doctors are under a duty to treat babies with Down's syndrome.

In the following case, the baby was dying and there was little that could be done for it. *Re C (A Minor) (Wardship: Medical Treatment)* (1989) concerned a baby who was born with fluid on the brain and who had a short life expectancy. The Court of Appeal said that, as the baby was both mentally and physically handicapped, 'the quality of her life will be demonstrably awful and intolerable', and it ordered that the hospital be allowed to treat the baby to relieve pain and suffering rather than to prolong its life.

The court examined what was relevant to 'best interests' in *Re J (A Minor) (Wardship: Medical Treatment)* (1990). J was born prematurely and suffered brain damage and often needed ventilation, although he was not dying. The likelihood was that he would be blind and deaf and unable to speak. The question arose as to what should be done if future ventilation was needed. The Court of Appeal, in exercising its wardship jurisdiction, took account of the fact that the child would have a poor quality of life; further ventilation may cause the child's condition to worsen; and ventilation was an invasive procedure for a baby. The doctors believed that it would not be in the child's best interests to ventilate him if he stopped breathing and the court agreed with this. Taylor LJ said that the three important principles which the courts follow are: (a) that they act in the best interests of the child; (b) respect for the sanctity of life imposes a strong presumption in favour of preserving it; and (c) the courts never sanction steps to terminate life. They try to look at the position from the point of view of the patient.

In these types of cases, the courts will not take on the role of telling doctors to give treatment against the medical judgment of the doctors; they tend to follow the wishes of the doctors. In *Re C (A Minor)* (1998), a 16 month old baby suffered from an incurable spinal disease. The doctors proposed stopping ventilation and, if there was a relapse, not e-ventilating. The parents were Jews and, although they agreed to stop ventilation, they wanted ventilation to be given in the future, if the baby needed it. The court allowed the hospital not to give treatment in the future. It would not make the hospital give treatment against the medical decision of the doctors.

Another difficulty is if a patient refuses to co-operate, so that treatment cannot be given. In *Re D (Medical Treatment: Mentally Disabled Patient)* (1998), the patient was a 49 year old man who had spent most of his life in psychiatric hospitals and lacked the capacity to consent. He needed kidney dialysis but, because he would not co-operate, the hospital gave him an anaesthetic each time he needed dialysis. The hospital sought a declaration that it was lawful not to give him treatment if he would not co-operate in the future. The court held that if, in the opinion of the doctors, it was not practicable to give him treatment, then it was lawful not to give treatment. This case can be contrasted with *Re JT (Adult: Refusal of Medical Treatment)* (1998), in which the patient, a 25 year old woman who lived in a mental hospital, suffered liver failure. She refused dialysis and said that she wanted to die. The court found that the patient *did* have mental capacity and, therefore, she could refuse treatment, so her refusal was binding on the hospital.

A more unusual situation is where the parents are in conflict with the wishes of the doctors and are against giving their child further treatment. In *Re T (A Minor) (Wardship: Medical Treatment)* (1997), a child was born with a liver defect and would die within two years without a transplant. The doctors believed that the operation was best for the child and that it was likely to be successful. Both parents were health professionals and were used to looking after sick children. They refused to consent to the transplant because of the pain and suffering that it would inflict on the baby. At first instance, the judge had granted the application by the doctors for the operation to be carried out and considered that the parents' opposition was unreasonable. On appeal, the Court of Appeal said that a number of factors had to be taken into account, including the wishes of the mother, who was against the operation; the fact that the baby had already had an unsuccessful operation to correct the liver problem; and the fact that the mother had gone to live abroad and would have to bring the baby back for the operation. Forcing the mother to agree would not be in the best interests of the child, as the mother would then have to look after the child, and the court refused to sanction the operation. This decision has been criticised Fox and McHale in 'In whose best interests?' (1997)

60 MLR 700, who point out that 'construing the mother and child a one permitted the Court of Appeal to minimise the potential conflic between the interests of the woman and child'. Was the decision in R T really in the child's best interests?

Mercy killing

Mercy killing is active euthanasia, and is the deliberate killing c someone. It will usually consist of killing a person who is terminally i and in great pain. In English law, this is murder. The fact that th defendant is acting from good motives is irrelevant. In *Airedale NH Trust v Bland* (1993), Lord Mustill stated:

> That 'mercy killing' by active means is murder ... has never, so far as I know, been doubted. The fact that the doctor's motives are kindly will for some, although not for all, transform the moral quality of his act, but this makes no difference in law. It is the intent to kill or cause grievous bodily harm which constitutes the *mens rea* of murder, and the reason why the intent was formed makes no difference at all.

In *R v Cox* (1992), Dr Cox injected his patient with a lethal substance i order to relieve her pain and Dr Cox was given a suspended sentence The courts usually take a sympathetic view where someone kills relative to put them out of their pain and such defendants are ofte convicted only of manslaughter: a person who carries out the merc killing of a member of their family has the defence of diminishe responsibility available, which has the effect of reducing the charge t manslaughter. However, it would be extremely unlikely for a doctor t be able to raise this defence. The suggestion of creating a separat offence of mercy killing, which would carry a maximum sentence c two years' imprisonment, was examined by the Criminal Lav Revision Committee in its *14th Report* in 1980. The Committee rejecte creating a new offence.

Permanent vegetative state

The 'permanent vegetative state' (or pvs) is a condition in which th cortex of the brain (the part responsible for thinking and the senses) i destroyed but the brain stem (which controls reflexive functions, suc as the heartbeat, breathing and digestion) continues to function. Suc a patient cannot communicate with the world and feels no pain. However, the patient in pvs is not dead.

In *Airedale NHS Trust v Bland* (1993), Tony Bland was crushed in the Hillsborough tragedy in 1989 and was diagnosed as being in pvs. He could still breathe but was fed liquified food through a naso-gastric tube. He had been in this state for nearly three years and it was accepted by medical staff that he would never become aware again. The hospital applied to the court for a declaration that they could withdraw life sustaining treatment, including feeding. The parents and doctors were agreed on this action. The House of Lords had to answer this question: in what circumstances, if any, could a hospital withdraw life sustaining treatment, with the result that the patient would die? The court said that there was a distinction between acts and omissions in law. If an act done with the intent to kill led to death, that was murder, but an omission with the same result was not an offence. There is an exception if a person is under a duty to act. Stopping artificial feeding was an omission, not an act, and could be seen as part of the doctor's duty of care to the patient.

The next question was whether the doctors were under a duty to continue to treat Tony Bland. Because he was not able to consent to treatment, he could only be treated, in accordance with *Re F* (1990), if the treatment was in his best interests. This had to be assessed by the '*Bolam* test' of whether such treatment was in accordance with 'a responsible body of medical opinion'. Here, it was in the patient's best interests that the treatment should be stopped and the court allowed this. The judges recognised that a point could be reached where there was no duty to continue to treat. Lord Browne-Wilkinson said that there could be a duty not to treat if:

> ... there comes a stage where the responsible doctor comes to the reasonable conclusion (which accords with the views of a responsible body of medical opinion) that further continuance of an intrusive life support system is not in the best interests of the patient, he can no longer lawfully continue that life support system: to do so would constitute the crime of battery and the tort of trespass to the person. Therefore, he cannot be in breach of any duty to maintain the patient's life.

In *Bland*, the court stepped beyond the existing boundaries in allowing passive euthanasia of patients in pvs.

The House of Lords also considered the procedure to be followed in situations where doctors wished to withdraw treatment from a patient in pvs. Sir Stephen Brown had said that a declaration should be obtained from the court in all cases of pvs. In the Court of Appeal, Sir Thomas Bingham MR said:

> This was in my view a wise ruling, directed to the protection of patients, the protection of doctors, the reassurance of patients' families and the reassurance of the public. The practice proposed seems to me desirable. It may very well be that, with the passage of time, a body of experience and practice will build up which will obviate the need for application in every case.

The House of Lords confirmed that this guidance should be followed. The Official Solicitor issued *Practice Note (Official Solicitor: Vegetative State)* (1996) 2 FLR 375, which sets out the procedure for applying to the court in such cases.

What is the position if the family objects to withdrawing treatment? In *Re G (Persistent Vegetative State)* (1995), a motorcyclist was injured in an accident and was diagnosed as being in pvs. Although his wife and the doctors wished to withdraw artificial feeding, his mother wished it to continue. The hospital applied to the court for a declaration to allow withdrawal of feeding. The court accepted that doctors should consult relatives about their views and that relatives may be able to give guidance on what the patient would want to do in the particular circumstances, but the views of relatives could not determine treatment. The declaration was granted and feeding was withdrawn.

In *Frenchay Healthcare NHS Trust v S* (1994), after taking an overdose of drugs, the patient was diagnosed as being in pvs. The patient was fed through a tube inserted through the stomach wall, but this tube became dislodged. Doctors believed that it would be against the patient's interests to insert another tube. The hospital obtained a declaration that it did not need to replace the tube. The Court of Appeal rejected the appeal, which was made on the ground that there should have been more time for an independent medical report to have been made. The court said that the patient had no prospect of recovery.

After the *Bland* case, a Select Committee of the House of Lords considered the issue of euthanasia (*Report of the Select Committee on Medical Ethics*, HL No 21, Vol I, 1994, HMSO). The Committee considered the arguments for euthanasia but was firmly against changing the law on intentional killing:

> That prohibition is the cornerstone of law and social relationships. It protects each of us impartially, embodying the belief that all are equal.

We do not wish that protection to be diminished and we therefore recommend that there be no change in the law to permit euthanasia.

The Committee also pointed out that legalising voluntary euthanasia would put pressure on the old and the sick to request death.

Bland has been criticised by a number of academics, including John Keown, who has said that the decision has left the law 'prohibiting active, intentional killing but permitting (if not requiring) intentional killing by omission, even by those under a duty to care for the patient' ('Restoring moral and intellectual shape to the law after *Bland*' (1997) 113 LQR 481).

The Medical Treatment (Prevention of Euthanasia) Bill 2000 provides, in cl 1, 'It shall be unlawful for any person responsible for the care of a patient to withdraw or withhold from the patient medical treatment or sustenance if his purpose or one of his purposes in doing so is to hasten or otherwise cause the death of the patient'. Clause 2 defines sustenance as 'the provision of nutrition or hydration, howsoever delivered'. The aim of this Bill is to stop patients having their lives ended by a deliberate omission such as withdrawing medical treatment or food and water. The effect of *Bland* was to allow passive euthanasia of some patients in pvs, and this Bill will change that position, if it is passed.

Refusal of consent to treatment

Competent patients

Can a competent patient refuse life saving treatment even if they know that doing so will lead to their death? In *Re T (Adult: Refusal of Medical Treatment)* (1992), the Court of Appeal said that a competent adult had the choice to accept or refuse such treatment. The courts are trying to maintain a balance between the interests of the patient and the interests of society in maintaining life. In *Bouvia v Superior Court of California* (1986), Bouvia was a mentally competent 28 year old but was completely paralysed, had arthritis and was in constant pain. She had a further life expectancy of 20 years. She refused food but doctors inserted a naso-gastric tube against her will. The court authorised removal of the tube, saying that Bouvia had the right to refuse life sustaining treatment. But does the patient intend to die, or are they simply intending to avoid the pain?

Patients who are no longer competent

If a patient decides, when competent, not to be treated if they develop certain conditions, do medical staff have to follow their wishes? The ethical principle of autonomy requires the wishes of such a patient to be followed, but is this the law? In North America, the concept of the 'advance directive' (or living will) has been established for some time. An advance directive is a statement, made when the patient is competent, setting out what treatment they want or do not want if they become incapacitated. If the patient specifies in the advance directive the treatment they would want, this is qualified to the extent that medical staff would decide whether such treatment was appropriate, as no one can demand a particular treatment. The case of *Malette v Shulman* (1990) is a clear example of how an advance directive works. There, a patient was taken to hospital, unconscious, after an accident. She was carrying a card which stated that she was a Jehovah's Witness and did not want a blood transfusion. Dr S gave a blood transfusion which saved her life. The court said: 'A doctor is not free to disregard a patient's advance instructions any more than he would be free to disregard instructions given at the time of the emergency.' The court added that a patient could reject treatment, even if to do so had harmful consequences. This was a battery and the doctor was liable to pay damages.

In English law, the legal status of an advance directive is unclear. The courts have accepted the idea of such advance directives and, in *Re T* (1992), Lord Donaldson MR commented that, 'if clearly established and applicable in the circumstances', they would bind the doctor. A *Practice Note* [1994] 2 All ER 413 states:

> The High Court exercising its inherent jurisdiction may determine the effect of a purported advance directive as to future medical treatment ... In summary, the patient's expressed views, if any, will always be a very important component in the decisions of the doctors and the court.

In *St George's NHS Trust v S* (1998), the court set out guidelines for medical staff to follow in dealing with patients who require invasive treatment. Part of these guidelines provide:

> (iii) Where the patient has given an advance directive, before becoming incapable, treatment and care should normally be subject to the advance directive. However, if there is reason to doubt the reliability of the advance directive (eg, it may sensibly be thought not to apply to the circumstances which have arisen), then an application for a declaration may be made.

The difficulties with advance directives include the following:

- does the statement cover the situation which arises? If if does not, then medical staff could ignore it;

- would the patient change their mind when in the actual situation which has arisen, if they could communicate? This leaves medical staff with the flexibility to ignore the advance directive;

- the actual wording of the directive may be unclear and open to different interpretations as to exactly what the patient wanted.

The Law Commission, in Report No 231, *Mental Incapacity* (1995), has proposed that legislation should be passed to give advance directives legal effect. The Commission did not want basic care, pain relief or feeding to be included. The Government has not included advance directives in their proposals for reform (see *Making Decisions*, referred to above, Chapter 2).

The British Medical Association's (BMA's) guidance, *Withholding and Withdrawing Life-Prolonging Medical Treatment* (1999), provides as follows:

> 10.1 Where a patient has lost the capacity to make a decision but has a valid advance directive refusing life-prolonging treatment, this must be respected.

The guidance explains that, if an advance directive names an individual whom the patient wishes the healthcare team to consult, this may be useful in making treatment decisions, although the wishes of that individual are not legally binding:

> 10.3 A valid advance refusal of treatment has the same legal authority as a contemporaneous refusal and legal action could be taken against a doctor who provides treatment in the face of a valid refusal.

The legal action contemplated would be a claim for battery.

If it is known that the patient would refuse treatment, but he has not explicitly said this, what is the position of medical staff? In the US, in such circumstances, the concept of 'substituted judgment' may be used. This means that a person (proxy) puts themselves in the position of the incapacitated person and makes a decision on the basis of what that person would have wanted, taking into account their knowledge of that person. In *Airedale NHS Trust v Bland* (1993), the House of Lords rejected the use of the substituted judgment test. One important limitation of such a test is that it can only be used if the patient has been competent at some time; they cannot make any choice for the permanently incompetent.

'Do not resuscitate' orders

A do not resuscitate (DNR) order is a direction which is put in the patient's notes, stating that the patient should not be resuscitated if their heart or lungs stop working.

In June 1999, a statement was issued by the BMA, the Resuscitation Council and the Royal College of Nursing, entitled *Decisions Relating to Cardiopulmonary Resuscitation*, which replaces earlier guidelines. They include the following provisions:

(1) DNR orders are appropriate if resuscitation is unlikely to be successful or is contrary to a competent patient's sustained wishes, or if resuscitation is not in accord with an advance directive, or where successful resuscitation is likely to be followed by a quality of life which is not in the best interests of the patient;

(2) if a DNR decision has not been made and the wishes of the patient are unknown, the resuscitation should be carried out;

(3) the responsibility for making the decision on DNR rests with the consultant or GP. The views of the health team, the patient, relatives and close friends may all be valuable in making the decision;

(4) where competent patients are at risk from cardiac or respiratory failure or have a terminal illness, the doctor should discover their wishes and document these in the patient's record;

(6) the decision in the records should also give reasons for the decision;

(8) decisions about DNR orders should be reviewed in the light of changes in the patient's condition;

(9) if the reason for a DNR order is that there will be no medical benefit, discussion with the patient should aim at obtaining an understanding and acceptance. If the patient cannot give a view, the views of family or close friends should be sought as to what the patient's views are believed to be.

The courts examined DNR orders in *Re R (Adult: Medical Treatment)* (1996), in which a 23 year old patient had cerebral palsy, malfunction of the brain, epilepsy and other ailments. He had a very low state of awareness and could not eat, but responded to pain and pleasure. He lived in a residential home and was taken to hospital, suffering from chest infections and fits. The consultant issued a DNR order, which the patient's mother agreed to. Staff at the day centre which the patient attended objected to this DNR order. The court considered the evidence that resuscitation might cause further brain damage and the chances of resuscitation being successful in a residential home were low. The court declared that withholding resuscitation and antibiotics was lawful.

In practice, the use of such orders has caused problems, with patients often being unaware that a DNR order has been made for them. There are still question marks over the involvement of patients and over decisions about the quality of life decisions for those patients.

The BMA's *Withholding and Withdrawing Life-Prolonging Medical Treatment* (1999) sets out detailed rules for healthcare staff in making decisions on treatment. The rules cover adults with capacity, advance directives, adults lacking capacity, children and young persons under 18.

The Human Rights Act 1998

In 'Do not resuscitate orders and the Human Rights Act 1998' (2000) 150 NLJ 640, Maclean considers the use of DNR orders made for old people without asking them. He argues that Arts 8, 2 and 14 of the European Convention on Human Rights may be relied on. Article 8 (respect for family life) was considered in *Gaskin v UK* (1989), where the European Court of Human Rights said that a child who was brought up in a local authority care home was entitled to see personal files about himself, because these contained information about his childhood and development. A failure to give individuals access to information about themselves was a breach of Art 8. Using this right would entitle a person to information about their treatment, for example a decision not to resuscitate them. This would not, however, give the patient the right to demand treatment, because of Art 8(2), which provides for exceptions. Under Art 2 (the right to life), the State has a duty to protect NHS patients in its care by doing what is reasonable (*Osman v UK* (2000)). Article 14 (freedom from discrimination) could operate if there was a blanket ban on treatment for older patients.

More generally, apart from the abovementioned Articles, Art 3, the right not to be subjected to inhuman treatment, may also be used by the families of patients kept on life support machines who wish the machines to be switched off. However, in *A NHS Trust v D* (2000), it was held that allowing doctors to withhold medical treatment, even involving a specific decision, was not a breach of Arts 2 or 3, provided that the decision was made in the best interests of the patient.

9 Property in the Body and Transplants

> **You should be familiar with the following areas:**
>
> - ownership of the body and parts of the body
> - transplants from dead bodies: Human Tissue Act 1961
> - live transplants: common law rules – competent, incompetent, children and pvs patients
> - live transplants: Human Organ Transplants Act 1989
> - xenotransplants
> - ways to increase supply: sale of organs; opting out; required request

Introduction

This chapter will examine issues surrounding ownership of the human body and parts of the body. The widespread practice of taking parts of children's bodies after their death for research purposes has highlighted some of the problems that the law faces, such as who has the legal right to bodies or body parts after death. The chapter will also discuss matters relevant to the transplant of organs from dead bodies, from live donors and from animals (xenotransplants). The first organ transplants took place in the 1950s, using kidneys, and a wide range of organs and tissue may now be transplanted. The transplant of organs and body tissues raises many ethical and legal issues and the law has lagged behind medical developments in this field. The demand for organs greatly exceeds the supply and there are over 5,000 patients waiting for an organ. Some believe that people should be able to sell their organs. From a Kantian perspective, others should not be used merely as a means to an end, and this would rule out transplants from live donors. The utilitarian approach would consider the overall benefits of transplants.

Property in the body

The question of whether someone can own their body raises difficult ethical and legal issues. As John Harris has pointed out, just because no one else owns my body, this does not mean that I do ('Who owns my body?' (1996) 16 OJLS 55). The concept of owning oneself is difficult to understand. The idea of ownership and property is a legal invention, which enables people to own things and to trade, and this latter activity underpins the working of society. Applying the concept of ownership to oneself seems alien. There is also the question of ownership of parts of the body. Many would frown on the idea of someone selling a part of their body, as this would not be treating their body with respect in accordance with the principle of autonomy. The idea of buying and selling bodily organs can be seen as treating parts of the body just like other goods. This is sometimes referred to as 'commodifying' the body.

The law has accepted that some regenerative parts of the human body may be classed as property. In *R v Welsh* (1974), the defendant was convicted of the theft of a urine sample he had given and, in *R v Rothery* (1976), the defendant was convicted of stealing a sample of blood he had given, which was to be tested for alcohol.

The Human Organ Transplant Act 1989 regulates live transplants and makes it a criminal offence to buy or sell organs (s 1). However, the Act does not deal with ownership of organs. The difficulties faced by courts dealing with this problem can be illustrated by the US case of *Moore v Regents of the University of California* (1990). Moore had leukaemia and his spleen was removed. Some of the cells from his spleen were used to develop new cells, which the doctor sold to a drug company. Moore did not know about this at the time and, when he found out, he sued for conversion, breach of fiduciary duty and lack of informed consent, the latter because he did not know what they were going to do with his cells. The court said that it was inappropriate to recognise property in the body for two reasons: (a) there were no precedents; and (b) it would hamper medical research, because the owner could then prevent others from using their tissue. They rejected the claim in conversion because Moore did not own this spleen. But the university was liable for breach of fiduciary duty and trespass. Even though Moore had no right to the cells developed, the university obtained a patent for them.

The Nuffield Report

The question of tissue ownership was considered by the Nuffield Council on Bioethics in Chapter 9 of *Human Tissue: Ethical and Legal Issues* (1995).

Someone from whom tissue is removed has no claim by statute: the Human Tissue Act 1961, the Human Organ Transplant Act 1989 and the Anatomy Act 1984 imply that tissue is given freely. At common law, the matter has not been decided, probably because tissue removed in the course of treatment is not wanted and tissue removed to give to others is a gift.

If tissue is removed in the course of an operation, the patient may be seen as abandoning it, and it is then in the possession of the hospital.

It could be argued that, when tissue is removed, it becomes the property of the patient. The patient may waive this right to it. In *Venner v State of Maryland* (1976), the court said that, when a person does nothing and says nothing about rights of ownership, the inference is he intends to abandon the material. Thus, there is a presumption in favour of abandonment. But, if the circumstances were such that abandonment could not be presumed, then, if no consent was given, property rights would not necessarily pass.

Another approach is to argue that, once tissue is removed, it becomes property but it is not owned by anyone until it is brought under dominion (that is, control), as with a wild animal.

The Nuffield Report then said that the approach of English law was unclear and suggested the following approach:

(a) any consent to treatment would imply that any tissue removed would be regarded as abandoned;

(b) any tissue removed for donation would be regarded as a gift. But if it was used for another purpose, this could lead to a claim;

(c) if tissue is removed with the intention of keeping it for the future use of the donor (for example, blood), the donor could claim that tissue. Note that embryos have their own statutory framework of consent;

(d) if tissue is removed without the explicit knowledge and consent of the patient, any claim over use will depend on the general consent given.

The Nuffield Report has been criticised by a number of writers, such as Mason and McCall-Smith, who say that it is based on the premise that people see no value in parts removed from their bodies: they point out that it is no longer true that parts cannot be valuable, for example, due to developments in biotechnology. The *Moore* case would be a classic example. The Report fails to deal with the right to own the parts of one's body.

What is the legal position as regards dead bodies and parts of dead bodies?

The original common law rule, as set down in *Dr Handyside's Case* (1749), was that there was 'no property in a corpse'. A recent case has qualified this rule. In *R v Kelly* (1998), the defendant and an accomplice stole various body parts from the Royal College of Surgeons. The defendant was an artist and wanted to use the parts in sculptures. They were both charged with theft and claimed that no one could own a dead body, so they could not be liable. The Court of Appeal said that the rule only applies to the corpse or parts of it which remain in their natural state. If parts of a corpse 'had acquired different attributes by virtue of the application of skill, such as dissection and preservation techniques, for exhibition and teaching purposes', then they were capable of being property. The parts taken had been used as specimens and the defendants were guilty of theft. The court added that the common law might recognise property in human body parts, even when those parts had not acquired different attributes, if they had attracted a 'use or significance beyond their mere existence', for example, as an organ transplant or for the extraction of DNA. As regards a corpse, the general rule was that the law recognises no property in a corpse. A corpse, or part of it, cannot be stolen. It is up to Parliament to change that principle.

If a right to body parts was recognised, who would have such a right? In *Dobson v North Tyneside HA* (1997), the claimant's daughter had died from a brain tumour and the claimant argued that the hospital had been negligent in not diagnosing the condition on time. The hospital had preserved the brain in paraffin and later disposed of it. It was also claimed that the hospital was liable in conversion for destroying the brain. The Court of Appeal held that there was no property in a corpse unless it had undergone a process of human skill, such as embalming. The preservation of the brain in paraffin was not on a par with embalming and the claimant had no right to possession of, or property in, the deceased's brain. Therefore, the claim in conversion failed. Neither did the claimant have the evidence to prove negligence. The court added that the executors have a limited right of possession of a corpse for the purposes of burial. The court approved the Australian case of *Doodeward v Spence* (1908), which concerned a two headed foetus which had been preserved in a jar. The High Court of Australia had said that, if someone does work on a corpse which is in their lawful possession which differentiates it from a corpse in its natural state, they acquire a right to possession, except for the claims of someone with a right to possession for the purpose of burial.

These decisions still leave questions unanswered. Do the executors have the right to return of the body and all the parts? Exactly what work needs to be done for a corpse or body part to become property? Kelly says that preserving something is sufficient.

Transplants

Transplants from dead bodies

At common law, the relatives of a deceased person have a right to the body for the purposes of disposal, but it is questionable whether this includes the right to donate organs from that body. In the early part of the 19th century, Burke and Hare dug up bodies and sold them to the Edinburgh Medical School, and then went on to murder people for the same purpose. It was only after their conviction for murder that the Anatomy Act 1832 was passed to regulate the use of dead bodies. This Act allowed people to give their body for medical purposes after their death. The law is now largely contained in the Human Tissue Act 1961, as amended by the Corneal Tissue Act 1986.

Section 1(1) of the Human Tissue Act 1961 provides that:

> If any person, either in writing at any time or orally in the presence or two or more witnesses during his last illness, has expressed a request that his body or any specified part of his body be used after his death for therapeutic purposes or for purposes of medical education or research, the person lawfully in possession of his body after his death may ... authorise the removal from the body of any part ... for use in accordance with the request.

Section 1(2) provides that the person in possession of the body may authorise removal of parts if, after making 'such reasonable enquiry as may be practicable', they have no reason to believe that:

- the deceased expressed an objection to his body being used; or

- a surviving spouse or relative objects to the use.

The above sub-sections mean that the deceased can allow removal of organs, or, if enquiry shows no objections from relatives, the hospital (or nursing home, etc) may authorise removal. The provision about making enquiries gives hospitals some degree of flexibility: where, for example, relatives cannot be contacted reasonably quickly, the hospital could allow removal.

The Department of Health's Code of Practice on *Diagnosis of Brain Stem Death – Including Guidelines for the Identification and Management of Potential Organ and Tissue Donors* (1998) provides that the person responsible for making enquiries has to 'make such reasonable enquiries as may be practicable'. In most situations, it is sufficient for doctors to discuss the matter of a transplant with a relative who had close ties with the deceased. The relative will be able to provide information on whether the family would object to a transplant. There is no need to establish a lack of objection from all relatives before authorising the removal of organs. The guidelines also state that, if the patient has a donor card or is on the Organ Donor Register, there is no need to ask the relatives if they object, although it is good practice to take their views into account.

Can children donate organs after their death? Presumably, a *Gillick* competent child could do so, although the point has not been decided.

Human Tissue Act 1961

Section 1(4) of this Act provides that the removal of parts must be carried out by a doctor, who must be satisfied 'by personal examination of the body that life is extinct'. An exception is made for eyes, which may be removed by other sufficiently qualified staff acting on the instructions of a doctor.

Section 1(5) provides that a coroner may stop an organ from being removed for transplant if the organ is needed as evidence.

Section 1(6) of the Act provides that no authority to remove parts may be given by someone who only has possession for the purpose of burial or cremation. This makes it clear that an undertaker who has possession of the body cannot give permission to remove organs.

Section 1(7) gives authority to managers of hospitals or other institutions where a body is lying to give permission for parts to be removed. This allows those in control of the institution to allow removal of body parts even though the dead person has not consented to this.

The Human Tissue Act 1961 does not provide any sanctions for its breach. Some arguments have been proposed that there could be liability in criminal law or the law of tort:

- Criminal law: in *R v Lennox Wright* (1973), the defendant obtained a job as a doctor, using forged qualifications. He removed eyes from a dead body and was charged with doing an act contrary to s 1(4) of the Human Tissue Act 1961 (before amendment of the Act, removal had to be carried out by a doctor). The court held that it was a common law offence to disobey a statute and the defendant was convicted. In the later case of *R v Horseferry JJ ex p IBA* (1987), the court said that, if there was no express provision in the Act for an offence, then it must be taken that Parliament did not intend to create one.

- Tort: a claim for nervous shock is a possibility if the requirements of *Alcock v Chief Constable of South Yorkshire Police* (1991) and *Page v Smith* (1995) are met. Claiming as a secondary victim could cause a difficulty with the requirement of the claimant seeing the event or its aftermath. The organ would not be removed in the presence of relatives, so they would have to see the body shortly afterwards.

Criticisms of the Human Tissue Act 1961

There are a number of problems with the meaning and effect of the Act. The phrase 'lawfully in possession of his body' has been taken to mean that, if the person dies in hospital, the hospital managers are in possession until the body is given to the executors, but there is an argument that the executors have the legal right to possession. The requirement for the hospital to make 'such reasonable inquiry as may be practicable' to see if the 'surviving spouse or any surviving relative' objects before removing organs has also caused difficulties. What is reasonable action here? If the spouse or relative objects, then the hospital has the right to remove the organ under s 1(1), but would be unlikely to do so. This effectively gives relatives a veto. But the Act does not take an unmarried partner into account. What is the position if the person has no relatives? Another difficulty is the fact that it is unclear whether there is any sanction for breach of the Act.

Beating heart donors

With transplants from dead bodies, the organ needs to be removed quickly before they degenerate through lack of oxygen. Some hospitals followed a practice of 'elective ventilation', whereby patients in a coma who suffered respiratory arrest were put on an artificial ventilator. This allowed the organs to be kept in good condition until the hospital was ready to transplant them. In 1994, the Department of Health issued guidelines stating that such practice was a battery, because it was not done in the best interests of the patient. Although these patients are 'brain stem dead', Mason and McCall-Smith, in *Law and Medical Ethics* (5th edn, 1999, Butterworths), say that there is opposition to such transplants because they appear to be taking organs from a living patient. They say that such fears are 'irrational' and suggest that issuing a death certificate before removing the organ would set the minds of relatives at rest.

Transplants from live donors

The common law

The rules dealing with transplants from living donors come from both the common law and statute. At common law, a person cannot consent to being killed or seriously injured. In *R v Brown* (1993), the court said that people could not give a valid consent to harming themselves. Distinctions may be made:

- between donating one of two kidneys, where the remaining kidney will keep the donor alive, and donating a single organ, such as the heart. Clearly, in the latter case, this would kill the donor and would not be allowed;

- between donating regenerative tissue (which can reproduce), such as bone marrow, and non-regenerative tissue, such as a lung. With regenerative tissue, donation will not harm the donor overall.

In 'The law relating to organ transplantation in England' (1970) 33 MLR 353, Gerald Dworkin set out three conditions for donation of an organ:

(a) the patient must give a free and informed consent – it is important to see that a patient is not donating under pressure from relatives;

(b) the operation must be therapeutic and for the patient's benefit – removing an organ from the patient can hardly be seen as for their benefit but it may be, psychologically, if they are donating it to their child;

(c) there must be a lawful justification – donating organs is seen as a benefit to society and can be justified.

Incompetent adults

An incompetent patient is not able to consent to donating an organ. Medical treatment may be given to an incompetent patient if it is in their 'best interests' (*F v West Berks AHA* (1989)). The difficulty is that donating an organ cannot easily be seen as being in the donor's best interests. The Law Commission, in its Report, *Mental Incapacity* (No 231, 1995), suggested that the donation of non-regenerative tissue by a mentally incapacitated person should automatically be referred to the court. They said that 'organ donation will only rarely, if ever, be in the best interests of a person without capacity, since the procedures and their aftermath often carry considerable risk to the donor'.

There have been some examples where donations have been allowed. In the US case of *Strunk v Strunk* (1969), the court allowed a kidney transplant from a mentally handicapped man with a mental age of 6 to his brother. The evidence was that he was very attached to his brother and if his brother died, this would affect him greatly. In *Re Y (Adult Patient) (Transplant: Bone Marrow)* (1996), Y was a physically and mentally handicapped 26 year old. She lived in a residential home. Her sister had a bone marrow disorder and wanted Y to be tested, with a view to donation of bone marrow. The court took into account the close relationship between Y and her mother and sister, who visited Y at the home, and the adverse effect that the death of the sister would have on Y. If the sister was not helped, she would have a much lesser chance from another donor. The mother would be left with a grandchild to look after and would have less time for Y. It was held to be in Y's best interests that the procedure should go ahead, because it would maintain and improve her relations with her mother and sister. Note that this case involved regenerative bone marrow and it remains to be seen if the English courts will follow *Strunk v Strunk*.

Children

Can a minor donate an organ? Such a procedure would not be treatment for the minor but would be for the benefit of someone else. If a child is young and is not *Gillick* competent, then it would require the consent of the parents to allow the child to donate an organ. Strictly, the parents can only give this consent if it is in the 'best interests' of the child. Following the approach of the courts in *Strunk v*

Strunk (1969) and *Re Y* (1996), it may be argued that donation to a sibling or parent could be in the child's best interests.

As regards children over 16, in *Re W* (1992), Lord Donaldson, speaking about s 8 of the Family Law Reform Act 1969, said that the Act only covered treatment and diagnosis and did not cover donating blood or organs:

> The doctor has a duty to act in the best interests of the patient. It is inconceivable [that] he should act in reliance solely on the consent of an under age patient, however *Gillick* competent, in the absence of supporting parental consent. He may be advised to apply to the court for guidance, as recommended by Lord Templeman in *Re B* (1987).

A particular difficulty with donations by children is to ensure that they are voluntary and not made under family pressure. Should children be allowed to donate organs to people other than close family members? As a general rule, this would be unlikely to be in the best interests of the minor and may allow exploitation of children.

Similar issues arise with minors receiving transplants. A *Gillick* competent child could consent but, in practice, a doctor would be unlikely to carry out a transplant without the consent of parents. Parents may refuse consent, as happened in *Re T* (1996), where the parents refused a liver transplant for a young baby.

The law on transplants and minors needs a set of clear rules, which will be of benefit to all those involved in such procedures. The British Medical Association (BMA) has said that 'only competent adults should be considered as live organ donors' (*Organ Donation in the 21st Century* – see below).

Patients in a permanent vegetative state (pvs)

These patients exist using their own heart and lungs and they are not brain stem dead. It has been argued by Hoffenberg, Lock, Tilney *et al* that waiting for them to die naturally after withdrawing feeding means that the organs will be useless for transplant. However, it is illegal to kill them. Nevertheless, by either changing the definition of death to include them or exempting pvs patients from the legal prohibition on killing, so that a lethal injection could be given, would have benefits. It would save the futile use of resources and would provide suitable organs for transplant. ('Should organs from patients in permanent vegetative state be used for transplantation?' (1997) *The Lancet* 1320.)

Statute

The law is contained in the Human Organ Transplants Act 1989. The Act was passed after Turkish nationals sold kidneys in the late 1980s and the transplants were carried out by surgeons in London. The Act defines 'organ' as 'any part of a human body consisting of a structured arrangement of tissues which, if wholly removed, cannot be replicated by the body' (s 7(2)). This distinguishes between parts of the body which can regenerate, such as blood, skin and bone marrow, and parts which cannot, such as kidneys, heart, liver and lungs. Only dealings in the latter are prohibited.

The main aim of the legislation is to prevent all commercial dealings in organs. Section 2(1) provides that it is an offence: (a) to remove an organ from a living person intended to be transplanted to another; or (b) to transplant an organ removed from a living person to another, unless the donor and donee are genetically related within the terms of s 2(2).

Under s 2(2):

... a person is genetically related to –

(a) his natural parents and children;

(b) his brothers and sisters of the whole or half blood;

(c) the brothers and sisters of the whole or half blood of either of his natural parents; and

(d) the natural children of his brothers and sisters of the whole or half blood or of the brothers and sisters of the whole or half blood of either of his natural parents ...

The relationship has to be proved by a genetic test under the Human Organ Transplants (Establishment of Relationship) Regulations 1989.

If a relationship cannot be established within the above requirements, then the transplant is treated as being between unrelated donors and various restrictions apply. Under the Regulations, the doctor responsible for the donor must refer the matter to the Unrelated Live Transplants Authority (ULTRA). Under s 2(3) of the Human Organ Transplants Act 1989, the Secretary of State may, by regulations, provide that the prohibition under s 2(1) does not apply in cases where no payment is made and the conditions in the Regulations are met. The Human Organ Transplants (Unrelated Persons) Regulations 1989 provide, under reg 3:

(a) no payment has been made;

(b) the doctor who referred the matter to ULTRA has clinical responsibility for the donor;

(c) the doctor has explained the nature of the procedure and the risks;

(d) the donor understands the nature of the operation and the risks;

(e) the donor's consent was not obtained by coercion or offer of payment;

(f) the donor understands that he can withdraw the consent;

(g) the donor and recipient have both been interviewed by a suitable independent person who confirms that the conditions have been met.

Section 1(1) of the 1989 Act makes it an offence to make or receive payment for an organ which is to be transplanted in Great Britain or elsewhere; or to agree to find someone willing to supply an organ for payment; or to initiate any arrangement for payment for an organ; or to take part in the management of any body involved in such arrangements. Section 1(2) makes it an offence to advertise for the supply of organs for payment and s 1(3) provides that 'payment' does not include costs and expenses of the donor in connection with the supply including loss of earnings.

One of the aims of the Human Organ Transplants Act 1989 was to prevent commercial dealings in live organs, which it achieves. The Act also distinguishes between related and unrelated donors and, with unrelated donors, rules have been put in place to ensure that such donors make the decision freely and without pressure. However, although the Act prevents payment to a related donor, it overlooks the fact that a related donor may be under various other pressures, for example, psychological pressure from their family to agree to donate an organ. It has been argued that all live donors should be protected. Recently, the BMA has said that 'all live donations should be subject to the same rigorous assessment, either by ULTRA or by some other mechanism, to ensure that the potential donation is truly voluntary and free from pressure' (*Organ Donation in the 21st Century: Time for a Consolidated Approach*, June 2000).

Liability for defective organs

If a transplanted organ is defective or carries a virus, the donee may be able to take legal action against the donor or the hospital. The possible claims would be in negligence or under the Consumer Protection Act 1987. A claim in negligence would most likely be taken against the hospital, as the donee would be unlikely to be at fault. The Consumer Protection Act 1987 imposes strict liability for damage caused by a defective product. There are a number of particular stumbling blocks in bringing such a claim. First, is an organ a 'product'? Although 'product' is defined in the Act as 'any goods', it has not been decided whether it includes organs. Secondly, the goods must be 'defective', which occurs if the safety is not such as persons generally are entitled to expect. The standard that donees are entitled to will depend on the organ being transplanted, the expertise available, etc. Thirdly, the Act makes the 'producer' liable and defines 'producer' as including the manufacturer, producer of raw materials and the processor. Can the donor, or the doctor who carried out the operation, or the hospital which acquired the organ, fall within this definition? It seems unlikely. Fourthly, under s 4(1)(e), there is a defence if a producer of such products could not have discovered the defect, given the state of scientific knowledge at the time. A hospital would have a good defence if it could show that the defect could not have been discovered.

Xenotransplantation

Xenotransplantation (or xenografting) is transplanting an organ from an animal to a human being. Research and experimentation on such transplants have been carried on for many years. Valves from pigs' hearts have been used successfully for humans since the 1960s and a number of transplants of animal organs have been attempted, but with no great success. In 1984, in the US, a baby was given a baboon's heart ('The Baby Fae case' (1987) 6 Medical Law 385) and survived for three weeks; since then, a range of organs from various animals have been transplanted.

There are two main areas of concern about this practice. First, there are scientific worries that humans reject such organs and that animal diseases could spread to humans. The development of immunosuppressant drugs and transgenic animals (which have human genetic material) results in less rejection. There are concerns that humans will contract animal diseases as a result of transplants. A man who was given a baboon's liver in Pittsburgh in 1992 contracted a virus from the baboon ((1999) *The Independent*, 1 October, p 13).

Secondly, there are ethical concerns about the use of animals for transplants. Is it morally acceptable to use animal organs for transplant into humans? From a utilitarian viewpoint, it is acceptable to use animals for such purposes if their suffering is outweighed by the benefit to people. Against this, many have argued that using animals for transplants causes them suffering, which outweighs any benefits to humans. Others say that we kill animals to eat, so using their organs is no worse than that. Downie ('Xenotransplantation' (1997) 23 J Medical Ethics 205) argues that there is a moral difference between eating animals, which is 'natural', because many animal species do it, and transplanting animal organs, which is 'unnatural', because only humans do it. Downie urges developing mechanical organs and improving the donation of human organs instead. Mason and McCall-Smith (*Law and Medical Ethics*) highlight the difficulties ahead if humans were to use animal brains and the cost of such procedures.

Two reports have been carried out on xenotransplants. The Nuffield Council of Bioethics issued a report entitled *Animal to Human Transplants: The Ethics of Xenotransplantation*, 1996. This report raised concerns about the use of primates for transplants because of their closeness in evolutionary terms to humans, and suggests the use of non-primates, such as pigs, instead. The risk of transmission of diseases is also pointed out. In 1997, a Government Advisory Group on Xenotransplantation, under the chairmanship of Ian Kennedy, said that the benefits to humans would outweigh the suffering to animals, which could be minimised. However, they recommended that no trials should take place for the present, because of the risk of diseases being transmitted to humans. There have not been any animal to human transplants in the UK.

How can the supply of organs be increased?

Three possible methods of acheiving this are suggested below.

(a) Allow the sale of organs

Under s 1 of the Human Organ Transplant Act 1989, buying or selling organs for transplant from live donors or from dead bodies is a criminal offence. It is argued that, if the sale of organs was permitted, this would increase the supply. Under the principle of autonomy, a person should be allowed to do what they want with their own body, including selling their organs. The sale of organs would help people who were dying.

But there are many arguments against selling organs:

- it would exploit of the poor, who would be the ones likely to sell;

- it would expose sellers to the risks and pain of the operation;

- allowing it would make body parts and, therefore, human beings seem like mere commodities;

- no one could give a truly voluntary consent to such a risky procedure;

- it would undermine the existing system of altruistic donation of organs as donors would want to be paid.

Some have argued in favour of allowing kidney sales: Radcliffe-Richards, Daar *et al*, in 'The case for allowing kidney sales' (1998) *The Lancet* 351, claimed that the arguments against the sale of kidneys are weak. One example of their argument is that the claim that it is risky to the seller must be set against people doing risky jobs for high pay or taking part in dangerous sports for pleasure. They say that a ban on sales is not justified, and are in favour of a controlled market of some sort.

The sale of organs from dead bodies would encourage relatives to agree to transplants, but raises fundamental concerns over our respect for the dead and how we treat dead bodies.

(b) A system of opting out

The current system under the Human Tissue Act 1961 is an 'opting in' one, under which people may carry a donor card, allowing their organs to be used on death, or they may register on the National Register in Bristol. This has not proved successful and a number of attempts have been made to change to a system under which individuals have to 'opt out' of donating their organs. This system is also known as 'presumed consent'. It is used in a number of European countries, including Italy, Spain and Belgium. There are some ethical concerns with this system, as the onus is on the individual to object and it seems like inertia selling. If individuals did not bother to register their objection, organs could be removed against their actual wishes.

(c) A system of required request

Under this system, medical staff would be under a legal duty to ask the relatives of the deceased patient for permission to remove organs. This system is used in the US. The evidence shows that such schemes are not very successful, partly because of the difficult position that medical staff face, in that they have to ask the relatives, who are already facing a traumatic situation, about removal of organs.

The Human Rights Act 1998

Article 2 (the right to life) could be invoked, but, as this requires a person only to do what is reasonable, it is unlikely to be a great help to patients needing transplants.

Article 14 (freedom from discrimination) could also be useful, for example, in the recent situation where the Great Northern Hospital in Sheffield accepted a donation of organs from a dead person on the condition that they would be used only for a white donee. The Human Tissue Act 1961 does not prohibit attaching conditions to the donation of organs but Art 14 could be invoked.

Reform of the system

In June 2000, the BMA set out its suggestions for reform of the transplant system in *Organ Donation in the 21st Century: Time for a Consolidated Approach*. It identified problems with the existing system, including difficulties with the interpretation of current legislation; the fact that the NHS Organ Donor Register had not been successful, in that less than 14% of the population had registered, it was not effective in keeping track of donors and it was not routinely checked when an organ was available; and the concern that organs would be removed before the patient was dead, which arose from confusion caused by the use of 'brain stem death'. They suggested that the term 'death confirmed by brain stem tests' would be clearer.

The BMA propose a system of presumed consent (opt out) and identified the Belgian system as a model. In Belgium, a register of non-donors is operated and people may register their objection at their local town hall. Additionally, an organ will not be taken if there is an objection from a close relative or spouse, unless that objection is contrary to the stated wishes of the deceased. The BMA wants a public debate and public support for the change to presumed consent.

It was also considered that elective ventilation was not realistic at present, because of practical and ethical difficulties. Some suggestions were rejected, including payment of live donors, that bodies should automatically be used for donation regardless of the wishes of the individual, required request and conditional donations.

The recommendations include:

- a single, comprehensive piece of legislation dealing with organ donation;

- up to date guidelines to determine death by brain stem tests before organs are removed;

- the removal of the distinction between related and unrelated live donors, with all live donations subject to the same assessment by ULTRA or other appropriate body;

- legal authorisation of invasive procedures after death to preserve organs;

- introduction of a system of presumed consent for adults.

Both the law on transplants and the system of procuring organs are in urgent need of reform. As the demand for organs continues to increase, but not the supply, many patients are left to die. The BMA's proposals deserve support.

Index